THE CATHOLIC UNIVERSITY OF AMERICA
CANON LAW STUDIES
No. 254

THE MASTER OF NOVICES

AN HISTORICAL SYNOPSIS
AND A COMMENTARY

BY THE

REV. JAMES FRANCIS LOVER, C.SS.R., M.A., J.C.L.
Priest of the Baltimore Province

A DISSERTATION

Submitted to the Faculty of the School of Canon Law of the Catholic University of America in Partial Fulfillment of the Requirements for the Degree of Doctor of Canon Law

THE CATHOLIC UNIVERSITY OF AMERICA PRESS
WASHINGTON, D. C.
1947

Imprimi Potest:

MICHAEL A. GEARIN, C.SS.R., J.C.D.,
Superior Provincialis.

Brooklynii, die 8 maii, 1947.

Nihil Obstat:

HIERONYMUS D. HANNAN, A.M., LL.B., S.T.D., J.C.D.,
Censor Deputatus.

Washingtonii, die 9 maii, 1947.

Imprimatur:

✠ MICHAEL J. CURLEY, D.D.,
Archiepiscopus Baltimorensis-Washingtoniensis.

Baltimorae, die 9 maii, 1947.

Printed by
THE PAULIST PRESS
401 West 59th Street
New York 19, N. Y.
81

TO

MY MOTHER

AND

FATHER

TABLE OF CONTENTS

PART II

CANONICAL COMMENTARY

CHAPTER III

CHAPTER IV

CHAPTER V

CHAPTER VI

CHAPTER VII

FOREWORD

THE importance and necessity of a Novice Master can hardly be exaggerated. For, since direction and instruction are necessary to attain any end, they are all the more necessary to attain the principal end and aim of the religious state: the achievement of perfection. Hence, a period of probation and training under the guidance of a competent director is necessary for candidates to the religious life. The spiritual welfare of both the novices and the religious Institute itself would otherwise be brought into jeopardy. It is no exaggeration therefore to say that the welfare and fate of a religious Institute rests in large measure in the hands of the Master of Novices.

The purpose of this dissertation is to trace the historical legal antecedents to the present legislation on the office of the Novice Master and, secondly, to give a commentary on the present legislation of the Code of Canon Law. The treatise is accordingly divided into two parts: a historical synopsis of the pre-Code legislation, and the commentary on the present law.

In view of the importance of the Novice Master, it is somewhat disconcerting to find that for a long while, up to the early seventeenth century, this office was a neglected point of law. This impression is tempered, however, by the realization that many matters affecting the religious life became points of law only after they had first been long-established customary practices prescribed by the religious rules themselves. It was only during the comparatively short period between the early seventeenth century and the promulgation of the present Code that the greater portion of legislation affecting the Novice Master was enacted.

In the commentary on the present law offered in the second part of this dissertation frequent reference is made to the Constitution *Cum ad regularem,* issued by Clement VIII on March 19, 1603, and frequent comparisons made between its stipulations and those of the current law. The reason for this is found not only in the fact that this Constitution was the first piece of complete and well-organized papal legislation affecting the Novice Master, but also because it is the chief source of the present law, the two being identical in most instances. To avoid unnecessary repetition therefore no detailed analysis of the Constitution is given in the historical section of this work. It was considered more appropriate to compare its requisites with those of the present law as each point of law is considered and commented upon.

The author welcomes this opportunity to thank his Provincial Superior, the Very Rev. Michael A. Gearin, C.SS.R., J.C.D., for the opportunity to pursue a course of graduate studies in canon law. He likewise expresses his sincere gratitude to the Faculty of the School of Canon Law of the Catholic University of America for their kindly, considerate and helpful assistance and for their many kindnesses over the past three years.

PART I

SYNOPSIS OF EARLY HISTORY

CHAPTER I

THE MONASTIC PERIOD

ARTICLE 1. THE MASTER OF NOVICES IN THE MONASTIC RULES OF THE EAST

A. The Hermits of St. Anthony (c. 251-356)

ST. ANTHONY'S (c. 251-356) traditional title, "Father of Christian Monks," though challenged by critics for a while, is now generally recognized by the historians of monastic origins.[1] Yet at first St. Anthony was a solitary living a life of strict enclosure in the Egyptian desert. Many others followed his example and, as the fame of his sanctity grew, began to settle near his own retreat. It was only at the insistence of these disciples that he undertook to organize and direct the multitude of monks that had gathered around him. This was about the year 305.[2]

There was no set rule of life governing these monks, each being left very much to himself and to his own discretion. The elders among them exercised an authority, but it was largely an authority of personal influence, a supremacy of greater spiritual wisdom. The younger monks put themselves under the guidance of a senior, and obeyed him in all things; but the bond between them was wholly voluntary.[3]

[1] Butler, *Benedictine Monachism* (2. ed., London: Longmans, Green and Co., 1924), p. 12.

[2] Butler, *The Lausiac History of Palladius* (Cambridge, 1898), p. 230.

[3] Butler, *The Lausiac History of Palladius*, p. 234.

B. The Rule of St. Pachomius (c. 328)

St. Pachomius (c. 286-346), "the founder of cenobitic monasticism,"[4] was the first of the early founders to establish rules for the training of aspirants to the common life. There were three distinct periods of religious training and instruction according to the Rule of St. Pachomius. First, the candidate asked for admission and was instructed in the rudiments of monastic discipline.[5] Secondly, there was a period of more thorough training under the guidance of a monk delegated by the superior for this work. However, this monk was not a novice master, but rather an instructor in letters.[6] Lastly, the spiritual instruction and direction of all the members of the community were given publicly by the *Praepositus*, that is, the Superior. These instructions were given three times a week, and the monks were obliged to discuss among themselves what they had learned from them. The monks could not be absent from these instructions without a very grave reason.[7]

By the time of Pachomius' death, about the year 346, his institute counted eight monasteries. In each monastery there were a number of separate houses, each with its own *Praepositus*.[8] It was the duty of the *Praepositi* to instruct the monks under their care, correct their faults, and watch over the *oblati*. Thus, according to the Rule of St. Pachomius the spiritual training of the monks was committed to the care of the Superior. It was not left to the zeal of the individual monks to seek out an instructor, as was the case with the Hermits of St. Anthony.[9]

[4] Altaner, *Patrologie* (Freiburg im Breisgau: Herder and Co., 1938), p. 162; Ladeuze, *Étude sur le Cénobitisme Pakhomien pendant le IVe Siècle et la première moitié du Ve* (Paris, 1898), p. 1. (Hereafter cited as *Le Cénobitisme Pakhomien.*)

[5] *Regula S. Pachomii*—Migne, *Patrologiae Cursus Completus, Series Latina* (221 vols., Parisiis, 1844-1864), XXIII, 70. (Hereafter this work will be cited *MPL.*)

[6] *Regula S. Pachomii—MPL,* XXIII, 78.

[7] *Regula S. Pachomii—MPL,* XXIII, 67, 85.

[8] Butler, *The Lausiac History of Palladius,* p. 235.

[9] *Regula S. Pachomii—MPL,* XXIII, 79, 83, 84, 85.

Since the newcomers received the chief portion of their instruction in the cenobitic life along with the rest of the community, it seems there was no formal novitiate among St. Pachomius' followers. However, the absence of a novitiate was corrected by the initial instructions on monastic life given previous to admission, as well as by the special surveillance to which the aspirants were submitted, and by the fact that the Superior could dismiss a member who did not live an edifying life. For these reasons it can be said there were adumbrations of a novitiate in Pachomian cenobitism, though as a formal and regular institution a novitiate did not exist.[10]

C. *The Rule of St. Basil* (c. 330-379)

St. Basil (c. 330-379) wrote two rules, but only in the longer one does he speak of the monk who had charge of the training and formation of the candidates. The Rule speaks of the *Praefectus* as the leader of the brethren in all things, and the one to whom an assistant was to be given for governing the community during the absence or sickness of the *Praepositus*.[11] However, the Rule of St. Basil is not very exact in determining the type of training that was to be given to the aspirants to the monastic life. Nor is it very specific which of the monks was to impart this training. Yet, the monk who performed this task does seem to have been distinct from the *Praepositus* or the Superior.[12]

Article 2. The Master of Novices in the Monastic Rules of the West

A. *Rule of John Cassian* (c. 360-430/35)

In the Rule written for his monastery in France, Cassian (c. 360-430/35) gives more explicit instructions for the novices than

[10] Ladeuze, *Le Cénobitisme Pakhomien*, p. 282.

[11] *Regulae Fusius Tractatae*—Migne, *Patrologiae Cursus Completus, Series Graeca* (161 vols., Parisiis, 1856-1866), XXXI, 987, 1031. (Hereafter cited as *MPG*.)

[12] *Regulae Fusius Tractatae:* "Praeficiatur autem talibus quispiam aetate provectior, caeterisque experientia praestantior."—*MPG*, XXXI, 954.

any of his predecessors. After the candidate's request for admission had been answered, he was first required to spend a full year under the care of the Senior in charge of guests and travellers.[13] Having persevered in this, the candidate was admitted to the community and put under the care of another Senior. Ten novices were committed to the care of this second Senior.[14] The importance of this office is clear from the wording of Cassian's Rule. The task of the Senior was to lead the young men to the heights of perfection. Cassian stressed the importance of imposing upon the novices tasks contrary to their natural inclinations. He likewise mentioned a manifestation of conscience which the novices were to make to the Senior in charge of them. They were advised to manifest their temptations to him, and not judge any thought good or evil until the Senior had passed judgment on it.[15]

B. Rule of St. Benedict (480-543)

The Rule of St. Benedict (480-543), fruit of the Roman genius for organization, gave to Oriental monasticism a form and pattern fitted to western conditions.[16] Indeed, it was the first monastic rule that can be called genuine legislation. Previous "rules" were but brief treatises on the monastic virtues with little orderly arrangement.[17] According to St. Benedict's Rule, a candidate seeking admission to the monastery was admitted to the guest's room only after he had patiently persisted to ask admission for four or five days. He then spent a few days in the guest room, and only after

[13] No profession is mentioned or supposed after the postulancy under the care of the first Senior. Hence the Senior who next took charge of the young men performed the function of a Novice Master.—cf. Van Espen, *Jus Ecclesiastium Universum* (5 vols. in 2, Coloniae Agrippinae, 1729), I, 156.

[14] *De coenobiorum institutis,* edited by Michael Petschenig in *Corpus Scriptorum Ecclesiasticorum Latinorum* (Vindobonae, 1866—), XVII, 52. (Hereafter this will be cited as *CSEL.*)

[15] *De coenobiorum institutis—CSEL,* XVII, 52.

[16] Altaner, *Patrologie,* p. 312.

[17] Ryan, *Irish Monasticism* (London: Longmans, Green and Co., 1931), p. 411.

this was he admitted as a novice and placed under the care of the senior member in charge of the novices.[18]

St. Benedict required that the Novice Master be one of the older monks and endowed with those virtues which were calculated to win souls. The Novice Master was obliged to devote himself to the novices. He was to exercise the greatest solicitude in examining each novice's aptitude for the monastic life, and in training him in monastic life and discipline. The purpose of this office was summed up by St. Benedict when he said the Master of Novices was to explain to the novices the arduous path that leads to God.[19]

If the monastic family was a large one, the Benedictine Rule provided for the appointment of deans who were to assist the Abbot in the government of the community.[20] These deans were sometimes called Masters of Novices, but it seems they were not such.[21] The question has been raised whether each novice had a Novice Master, or whether there was but one Master deputed to take charge of the entire group of novices. Abbot Haeften (+1648) inclined toward the opinion that each novice had a separate Master.[22] However he furnished little evidence to prove this point, and indeed there are good reasons supporting the opposite view.

In the first place, had there been a Novice Master for each novice, a general mingling of the professed members and the novices would have resulted. Yet it was precisely to offset this that the

[18] Butler, *Sancti Benedicti Regula Monasteriorum, Editio Critico-Practica* (editio altera, Friburgi Brisgoviae, 1927), cap. LVIII. (Hereafter this will be cited *Regula Sancti Benedicti.*) Commenting on this passage, Van Espen says: "Senior, cuius hic meminit Benedictus, est ille, qui hodie appelatur *Magister Novitiorum."—Jus Ecclesiasticum Universum,* I, 156.

[19] "Et senior eis talis deputetur qui aptus sit ad lucrandas animas, qui super eos omnino curiose intendat. Et sollicitudo sit si revera Deum quaerit, si sollicitus sit ad Opus Dei, ad oboedientiam, ad obprobria. Praedicentur ei omnia dura et aspera per quae itur ad Deum."—*Regula Sancti Benedicti,* cap. LVIII; cf. Martène, *Regula S.P. Benedicti commentata—MPL,* LXVI, 813.

[20] *Regular Sancti Benedicti,* cap. XXI.

[21] Martène, *Regula S.P. Benedicti commentata,* cap. XXI.—*MPL,* LXVI, 485.

[22] *S. Benedictus illustratus, sive disquisitionum monasticarum libri XII, quibus S.P. Benedicti regula religiosorum rituum antiquitates varie dilucidantur* (Antverpiae, 1644), lib. IV, tract. IV, disq. 1.

novices were assigned their own special quarters within the monastery. Moreover, it would have been difficult to find a sufficient number of professed members possessing the qualities required of a Novice Master, particularly an advanced age and outstanding ability in the art of directing souls.[23]

Furthermore, an examination of the ancient monastic rituals of profession shows that they invariably spoke of a single Novice Master charged by the Abbot with the religious formation of the entire group of novices.[24] Therefore, the presumption that St. Benedict in his Rule followed the practice of the monks of Egypt, who committed a group of ten novices to one Master, is entirely warranted.[25]

Finally, it may reasonably be argued that in this regard St. Benedict would be expected to follow the prescriptions of Cassian, to whom, among his monastic sources, he was most indebted.[26]

C. Rule of St. Columbanus (c. 540-615)

The *Regula Monachorum* [27] of the great Irish monk, St. Columbanus (c. 540-615), gave an extraordinary impetus to the growth of monasticism. It was followed in a great many monasteries throughout seventh-century Gaul, but especially at the monasteries of Luxeuil in France and of Bobbio in Italy, both of which Columbanus himself had founded and in which he had lived.[28]

Though widely accepted and long retained, the Rule of Columbanus was not as detailed and explicit as was that of St. Benedict. For example, Columbanus' Rule mentions nothing of a novitiate or

[23] Martène, *Regula S.P. Benedicti commentata—MPL,* LXVI, 813.

[24] Martène, *De Antiquis Ecclesiae Ritibus* (4 vols. in 3, Rotomagi, 1700-1702), III, lib. II, cap. II, *de benedictione monachorum; idem, Veterum scriptorum et monumentorum moralium, historicorum, dogmaticorum collectio nova* (Parisiis, 1700), I, 297.

[25] *S. Benedicti abbatis anianensis concordia regularum—MPL,* CIII, 1264; Van Espen, *Jus Ecclesiasticum Universum,* I, 156.

[26] Butler, *Benedictine Monasticism,* p. 165; Altaner, *Patrologie,* pp. 290-291.

[27] Edited by O. Seebass—*Zeitscrift für Kirchengeschichte* (Gotha, 1880—), XV (1895), 366-386.

[28] Kenney, *The Sources for the Early History of Ireland* (2 vols., New York: Columbia University Press, 1929), I, *Ecclesiastical,* p. 188.

of a Novice Master. Consequently it was gradually eclipsed by the more practical rule, until eventually the Rule of St. Benedict triumphed everywhere.[29]

At first the Benedictine Rule was adopted side by side with that of Columbanus, then substituted for it, and at length it totally and everywhere supplanted it.[30] The two chief reasons for the success of Benedict's Rule over that of Columbanus were, first, that St. Benedict's Rule gained early favor at Rome,[31] and, secondly, that the Benedictine Rule was not only more thorough and definite in its construction, but also more moderate and prudent in its demands than was the severe, penitential Rule of St. Columbanus.[32]

[29] Montalembert, *Saint Columban,* critical edition: E. J. McCarthy (St. Columbans, Nebraska, 1927), p. 136.

[30] Kenney, *The Sources for the Early History of Ireland,* I, 188; Montalembert, *Saint Columban,* p. 138.

[31] Only a short while after its original approval by Gregory the Great in 595, Boniface IV in a Council of Rome, held in 610, spoke of St. Benedict as "the legislator of the monks" (*monachorum praeceptor*).—Mansi, *Sacrorum Conciliorum Nova et Amplissima Collectio* (53 vols. in 60, Parisiis, Arnhem, Lipsiae, 1901-1927), X, 503. (Hereafter this work will be cited as Mansi.)

[32] Montalembert, *St. Columban,* pp. 137, 142.

CHAPTER II

FROM THE MONASTIC PERIOD TO CLEMENT VIII (1592-1605)

THOUGH the early monastic rules were not very explicit and detailed in providing for a Master of Novices, still there are definite traces of the office throughout the monastic period. During the period between the early monastic rules and the beginning of the seventeenth century there was little or no canonical legislation on the office of the Master of Novices. Detailed legislation was enacted only in 1603, when Clement VIII (1592-1605) issued his Constitution *Cum ad regularem.*[1] Therefore for the period previous to the enactment of this Constitution the general legislation on the novitiate will be presented. Legislation on this accepted institution in the religious life necessarily affects the Master of Novices to some degree.

ARTICLE 1. LEGISLATION OF THE EARLIER COUNCILS

During the period of the rise of monasticism conciliar legislation contributed little to the development of the novitiate, and practically nothing to the office of the Novice Master. The Council of Chalcedon (451) mentioned the reception of candidates, but did not require a definite period of training.[2]

The II Council of Toledo (527/531)[3] required that those young men who from infancy were dedicated by their parents to the clerical state should be tonsured and live under the surveillance of the bishop and a deputed superior. It is of note that in the annotations of the *Correctores Romani* it is stated that in all the older editions of the councils and in the two Vatican codices of the coun-

[1] 19 mart. 1603—*Codicis Iuris Canonici Fontes,* cura Emi Petri Card. Gasparri editi (9 vols., Romae [postea Civitate Vaticana]: Typis Polyglottis Vaticanis, 1923-1939.—Vols. VII, VIII, et IX cura et studio Emi Iustiniani Card. Serédi), n. 189. (Hereafter cited as *Fontes.*)

[2] Can. 4—Mansi, VII, 394; Bruns, *Canones Apostolorum et Conciliorum Saeculorum IV-VII* (2 vols., Berolini, 1839), I, 26-27. (Hereafter this will be cited as Bruns.)

[3] Can. 1—Bruns, I, 207-208; cf. *Decretum Gratiani,* c. 5, D. XXVIII.

cils this law likewise applied to those dedicated to the religious life—"in clericatus officio, vel monachali (al. monachi) posuit." However this reading is given neither by Gratian nor by Bruns.

An enactment of the IV Council of Toledo (633), though it does not refer to the Master of Novices, may be regarded as a piece of legislation parallel to the requirement of a Novice Master as embodied in St. Benedict's Rule. The Council prescribed that young clerics ("inpuberes aut adolescentes") be placed in the care of an upright older cleric who was to be their instructor and also a witness of the probity of their conduct.[4]

The first general law requiring a novitiate before profession of vows was enacted by the IV General Council of Constantinople (869). The law established a probation period of three years. However, if the novice was already known in the monastery, or if he fell gravely ill, a novitiate of six month sufficed.[5]

Article 2. Law of the Decretals

In the Decretal Law of the Popes as presented by Gratian there is no mention at all of the office of the Master of Novices, though there is considerable legislation on the novitiate.[6] This does not argue for the non-existence of the office of Novice Master, but rather indicates that it was an accepted institution in the religious life governed more by monastic custom than by canonical legislation. Among other points relating to the novitiate, Gratian quoted Alexander II (1061-1073) to the effect that no one was to be professed as a monk before a full year of probation.[7]

[4] Can. 24: "Omnes . . . in disciplinis ecclesiasticis agant, deputati probatissimo seniori, quem et magistrum doctrinae et testem vitae habeant."—Bruns, I, 231; Gratian likewise embodies this in his *Decretum*—c. 1, C. XII, q. 1.

[5] Can. 5—Mansi, XVI, 539.

[6] For a summary of the Decretal Law on the novitiate cf. Thomassinus, *Vetus et Nova Ecclesiae Disciplina* (3 vols., Venetiis, 1730), pars 1, lib. III, cap. XLVIII.

[7] C. 1, C. XVII, q. 2; cf. Jaffé, *Regesta Pontificum Romanorum, ab condita Ecclesia ad annum post Christum natum* 1198 (editionem secundam correctam et auctam auspiciis Gulielmi Wattenbach curaverunt S. Loewenfeld, F. Kaltenbrunner, P. Ewald, 2 vols. in 1, Lipsiae, 1885-1888), n. 4625 (3525), (hereafter cited as *Regesta*); also Mansi, XIX, 960.

In the second part of the *Corpus Iuris Canonici* there is included a law, issued by Innocent III (1198-1216), forbidding religious profession to be made before the completion of the novitiate.[8] Boniface VIII (1294-1303) extended the *privilegium canonis* to novices, although novices were not religious in the strict sense of the term. Thus those who laid violent hands on a novice suffered the penalty of excommunication *latae sententiae*.[9]

In the entire *Corpus Iuris Canonici* the only direct reference to the Master of Novices is found in the decretals of Clement V (1305-1314).[10] The law merely stated that a competent instructor shall be assigned to instruct the novices in the divine offices as well as in the regular observances.[11] It is fairly certain that the decree in which this reference appears was of a conciliar character, having been issued by the Council of Vienne (1311-1312).[12]

Originally the decree aimed at the reform of Benedictine monastic life. But, since it was embodied in the decrees of Clement V, it obtained universal legal force when the *Decretales Clementinae* were officially promulgated by Pope John XXII in 1317. The Synod of Rouen (1335) renewed this decree and ascribed it to the Council of Vienne.[13] The Synod of Valladolid (1322) likewise renewed it, but spoke simply of a constitution of Clement V.[14]

[8] C. 16, X, *de regularibus et transeuntibus ad religionem*, III, 31.

[9] C. 21, *de sententia excommunicationis, suspensionis et interdicti*, V, 11, in VI°.

[10] C. 1, *de statu monachorum vel canonicorum regularium*, III, 10, in Clem.

[11] "Novitiis etiam fidelis deputetur instructor tam in divinis officiis quam in observantia regulari."—The gloss on this sentence stresses the need of the Master's orthodoxy in these words: "fidelis, non solum catholicus, sed etiam diligens, et fidelis et legalis." (Joannes Andreae.)

[12] Schroeder, *Disciplinary Decrees of the General Councils* (St. Louis: B. Herder Book Co., 1937), p. 413.

[13] Can. 3—Mansi, XXV, 1041; Hefele-Leclercq, *Histoire des Conciles* (10 vols. in 19, Paris: Librairie Letouzey et Ané, 1907-1938), VI, pars 2, 836.

[14] Cap. XII—Mansi, XXV, 707.

Article 3. Rules

The development of Monasticism in the West owed much to the universal character with which St. Benedict had endowed his Rule.[15] Explicitly approved by Gregory the Great in the II Council of Rome (595),[16] St. Benedict's Rule became almost the only rule in some parts of Europe in the ninth century.[17] Not only monasteries of male religious, but likewise many monasteries of women religious followed it.[18] Indeed it became supreme all over Europe, and eventually supplanted the other systems of monasticism, notably that of St. Columbanus, in places where they had long been in force.[19] It can rightly be said therefore that the Rule of St. Benedict kept pace with the Church of Rome itself.[20]

Previous to the introduction of the Benedictine Rule, monasteries had been governed by custom and not by law, a great deal of latitude having been given to the Abbot.[21] But with the introduction of Benedict's Rule all this was changed; many things formerly governed by custom were definitely fixed by legal enactments.[22] Hence the Rule of St. Benedict can be regarded as the initial step towards a universal enactment on many points of monastic life, the novitiate and the Master of Novices among them.

[15] McLaughlin, *Le très ancien droit monastique de l'Occident* (Paris: Picard, 1935), p. 16; Berliere, *L'ordre monastique des Origines au XIIe siècle* (3. ed., Paris, 1924), p. 27.

[16] Mansi, X, 476-477.

[17] Council of Châlon-sur-Saône (813), c. 22: "Paene omnia monasteria regularia in his regionibus constituta secundum regulam sancti Benedicti se vivere fatentur; quae beati Benedicti documenta per omnia demonstrant, qualiter eis vivendum sit."—*Monumenta Germaniae Historica* (Inde ab anno Christi quingentesimo usque ad annum millesimum et quingentesimum, edidit Societas Aperiendis Fontibus Rerum Germanicarum Medii Aevi) *Legum Sectio* III, Tom. II, (*Concilia*), pars I (ed. A. Werminghoff, Hannoverae, 1906), p. 278.

[18] Leclercq, "Monachisme"—*Dictionnaire d'archéologie chrétienne et de liturgie* (14 vols., Paris: Librairie Letouzey et Ané, 1907—), XI, 1921-1922.

[19] Ryan, *Irish Monasticism*, p. 412.

[20] Montalembert, *Les moines d'Occident* (6. ed., 7 vols., Parisiis, 1878-1882) II, 644-645.

[21] Ryan, *Irish Monasticism*, p. 411.

[22] Ryan, *Irish Monasticism*, p. 412.

According to the Benedictine Rule[23] parents were allowed to dedicate their children as oblates in the monastery. This practice was continued at the famous monastery at Cluny. When fifteen years old, these *oblati* could be admitted as novices if the chapter had decided they were fit. They were then put under the care of the Master of Novices for their novitiate training, which was concerned chiefly with the ways of the monastic life and with the spiritual development of the novices.[24]

There is no express mention of a Novice Master in the statutes of the monastery at Cluny, though it might be argued that a Senior was put in charge of the novices, since the Rule of St. Benedict required this, and the monks at Cluny followed the Benedictine Rule. However, this argument does not seem valid as regards the novitiate, for it seems from the statutes that a month was regarded sufficient, though the Benedictine Rule required that a novitiate last a full year.[25]

In the *Charta Charitatis,* the first constitution of the Cistercian Order, no mention was made of the Novice Master. It was merely briefly stated that the members were to follow the Rule of St. Benedict.[26] But in the *Usus Antiquiores Ordinis Cisterciensis* the Novice Master was directed to instruct his novices, correct their faults, administer penances and see that they were provided with the necessities of life.[27]

With the rise of the Cistercian monastery at Citeaux during the twelfth century a number of important innovations were made. They were first made in practice and later embodied in legislation. One requirement was that a year's novitiate was demanded of aspirants to the monastic life. Strictly, this was no innovation, but rather a return to the Benedictine Rule. But since the contrary practice had become so normal at Cluny and at other monasteries, it had all

[23] *Regula Sancti Benedicti,* cap. LIX.

[24] Evans, *Monastic Life at Cluny* 910-1157 (London: Oxford University Press, 1931), pp. 47-49.

[25] *Statuta Congregationis Cluniacensis—MPL,* CLXXXIX, 1036.

[26] *Charta Charitatis—MPL,* CLXVI, 1379.

[27] *Usus Antiquiores Ordinis Cisterciensis—MPL,* CLXVI, 1491-1492.

the appearances of an innovation. Oblate children were forbidden in the monastery, and an age of sixteen years was established as the minimum age for entrance into the monastery.[28]

There is some evidence to show that at least in England among the Black Monks the Novice Master did little more than teach the customs of the house and watch over the external deportment of his charges. Among the White Monks the Master was required to give spiritual formation as well.[29] The monastery at Citeaux instituted a reform of the novitiate and gave it an importance it had ceased to have among the Black Monks. The Cistercians made it a year of real probation and training, and the Novice Master was assigned a position of importance immediately after the Superior.[30]

Two constitutions of Benedict XII, *Fulgens sicut stella* (1335),[31] which established norms for the reform of the Cistercian Order, and *Summi Magistri* (1336), which regulated the reform of the Black Monks of St. Benedict,[32] speak of the qualities the candidates must have before admission to the novitiate; but of the novitiate itself only general terms are used, and nothing at all is said of the Novice Master.

With the rise of the mendicant orders in the twelfth and thirteenth centuries nothing new concerning the Novice Master was introduced. As regards the Friars Minor, there was no novitiate at all in their very early days, until 1220, according to Huber.[33] However, in the document presented by Huber as the first rule of the Friars Minor (1209-1221) a year of probation is expressly mentioned, though there is no mention of a Novice Master.[34] The first

[28] Knowles, *The Monastic Order in England* (Cambridge: The University Press, 1940), p. 212.

[29] Knowles, *The Monastic Order in England,* p. 422.

[30] Knowles, *The Monastic Order in England,* pp. 634, 637; *Usus Antiquiores Ordinis Cisterciensis—MPL,* CLXVI, 1491.

[31] *Bullarum Diplomatum et Privilegiorum Sanctorum Romanorum Pontificum Taurinensis Editio* (25 vols., Augustae Taurinorum, 1857-1872), IV, 337. (Hereafter cited as *Bull. Rom.*)

[32] *Bull. Rom.,* IV, 376-378.

[33] Huber, *A Documented History of the Franciscan Order, 1182-1517* (Milwaukee: The Nowiny Publishing Apostolate, 1944), pp. 17; 267.

[34] Huber, *A Documented History of the Franciscan Order,* p. 606.

rule was approved by Innocent III in 1209 or 1210, though the Bull of approval is not extant.[35] In the second rule of the Friars Minor, approved by Honorius III in 1223, by virtue of the Bull *Solet annuere,*[36] a year of probation was again expressly required, but still there was no mention of a Novice Master.[37]

The first explicit mention in the Franciscan Rule of the Novice Master and his qualifications seems to have come with the new constitutions issued for the Friars by Benedict XII, in 1336, in the Bull *Redemptor noster.* In each province certain designated monasteries were to be places for the training of the novices. The Provincial Minister or his substitute was to assign as Novice Master a mature and discreet friar, who was to give his continual attention to the novices, instructing them in the ways of God, allowing them to confess frequently, and teaching them both by word and by example the customs and religious observances of the Order.[38]

Among the Dominicans it was the duty of the Prior to place a Novice Master over the novices. However, the Rule of St. Dominic added nothing new to the Master's duties. It was merely repeated that he was to instruct the novices in the customs of the Order and to lead them in the ascetical life, teaching them especially to confess frequently.[39]

Article 4. The Council of Trent (1545-1563)

Of the Master of Novices the Council of Trent made no mention. However, in the fifteenth chapter of Session XXV, concerning regulars and nuns, it did decree that in no religious order what-

[35] Huber, *A Documented History of the Franciscan Order*, pp. 13-14.

[36] *Bull. Rom.*, III, 394.

[37] Huber, *A Documented History of the Franciscan Order*, p. 627.

[38] "In quolibet illorum conventuum magistrum novitiorum assignet unum in eadem religione probatum, maturum, devotum, providum et discretum, qui huiusmodi novitiorum continuam curam gerat, viam Dei ipsos doceat, saepe et pure eos confiteri faciat, et ad servandam cordis et corporis puritatem informet, mores et observantias eiusdem religionis eis verbo et exemplo demonstret."—*Bull. Rom.*, IV, 392, 393.

[39] Galbraith, *The Constitutions of the Dominican Order* (Manchester: The University Press, 1925), Appendix II, cap. XIV, p. 215.

ever, whether of men or of women, was profession to be made before the completion of the sixteenth year, and no one was to be admitted to profession who had been under probation less than a year after the reception of the habit.[40] In the two following chapters of the same session the Council made regulations concerning the property of the novices, and gave universal force to the institution of the *exploratio voluntatis*.[41]

Article 5. The Constitution of Clement VIII, *Cum ad Regularem,* March 19, 1603

Canonical legislation on the Master of Novices was very meager prior to the early seventeenth century. Still, it is none the less true that the office of Novice Master was known, and that the functions of the office were performed even in the early beginnings of the monastic life, though the name may not have been known, and the duties of the senior monk in charge of the training of the novices may not have been as detailed and determined as they later became. Thus it was more by monastic custom than by legal enactment that the institution of the Master of Novices developed. But with the turn of the seventeenth century there began a new era of legislation in the history of the constitution and development of the novitiate and of the Novice Master as canonical institutes. The chief and most important factor, as regards the office of the Master of Novices, was the promulgation of the papal Constitution *Cum ad regularem* by Clement VIII on March 19, 1603.[42]

This Constitution was the first definite, clear-cut and detailed legal enactment on the office of the Novice Master. It may well be regarded the link between the very early monastic practices and the present day law on the office of the Novice Master. For it was the long-standing monastic customs and practices that, in large meas-

[40] *Canones et Decreta Sacrosancti et Oecumenici Concilii Tridentini* (Editio Novissima ad Fidem Optimorum Exemplarium castigate Impressa, XIX Reimpressio Stereotypa, Taurini, 1913), Sess. XXV, *de regularibus,* c. 15.

[41] Sess. XXV, *de regularibus,* cc. 16, 17.

[42] *Fontes,* n. 189.

ure, formed the basis for Clement's constitution, while on the other hand it became itself, in turn, the basis for the present canonical law on the office of the Master of Novices.[43]

The organization of the novitiate, then, was accomplished chiefly through the Constitution *Cum ad regularem.* In issuing this law Clement VIII renewed the laws made for religious by his predecessors Sixtus V [44] and Gregory XIV.[45] But more important still, this Constitution regulated in great detail the reception and the training of the novices. Prompted by a desire to have regular observance and discipline flourish in every monastery, and to offset any laxity in the reception and the training of the novices, the Pope by means of this Constitution sought to supplement the canons and decrees of the Council of Trent, the legislation of the previous Pontiffs, and the provisions of the constitutions of the various Religious Orders and Institutes.[46]

Originally this Constitution applied only to monasteries in Italy and the adjacent islands. However, in 1624, through a decree of the Sacred Congregation of the Council, Urban VIII (1623-1644) renewed and solemnly confirmed the Constitution *Cum ad regularem.*[47] The intention of this decree, so it seems, was to extend the Constitution of Clement VIII in order to give it universal force binding on all regulars everywhere. Many authors upheld this contention.[48] Other authors maintained that it could not be proved conclusively that the

[43] "Clément VIII a exprimé la tradition de l'Eglise et toutes les saintes inspirations des fondateurs des congrégations religieuses dans la celebre décret du 19 mars 1603, que le pape Urbain VIII promulgua de nouveau de la manière le plus solennelle le 26 octobre 1624."—*Analecta Juris Pontificii* (Romae, 1855-1869; Parisiis, 1872-1891), V (1861), 182. (Hereafter cited as *AJP.*)

[44] Const. *"Cum de omnibus,"* 26 nov. 1587—*Fontes,* n. 162; const. *"Ad Romanum,"* 21 oct. 1588—*Fontes,* n. 164.

[45] Const. *"Circumspecta,"* 15 mart. 1591—*Fontes,* n. 170.

[46] Clemens VIII, const. *"Cum ad regularem,"* 19 mart. 1603, §§ 1, 2—*Fontes,* n. 189.

[47] S.C.C., decr. 21 sept. 1624, § 1—*Fontes,* n. 2454.

[48] Giraldi, *Expositio Iuris Pontificii* (2 vols., Romae, 1769), pars I, sectio DXXXIV; De Angelis, *Praelectiones Iuris Canonici* (2. ed., 5 vols., Romae, 1908), lib. III, tit. XXXI, n. 8; Santi-Leitner, *Praelectiones Juris Canonici* (4. ed., 3 vols., Ratisbonae, 1903-1905), lib. III, tit. XXXI, n. 17.

Constitution *Cum ad regularem* had been given universal force through the decree of the Sacred Congregation of the Council.[49] The latter seems to have been the proper interpretation in view of the fact that the Sacred Congregation of Bishops and Regulars declared that the Constitution *Cum ad regularem* applied only to Italy even after Urban VIII had renewed and confirmed it.[50]

Yet, even though the Constitution *Cum ad regularem* was not a universal law, and although it applied strictly only to regulars, still its prescriptions were an excellent norm for the government of all novitiates and for the training of all novices.[51] Because it was such an excellent norm and guide, it was everywhere observed as the code of the novitiate for regulars, and the Sacred Congregation of Bishops and Regulars in approving Congregations of simple vows always gave its prescriptions in accord with those of the Constitution *Cum ad regularem.*[52] The debate about the universal force of the Constitution *Cum ad regularem* was therefore of little moment. For since the Constitution was actually observed everywhere as a guiding principle, it exercised an important influence in the organization and government of the novitiate.

[49] Wernz, *Ius Decretalium* (2. ed., 6 vols., Romae et Prati, 1906-1913), III, 309, note (262); Vermeersch, *De Religiosis Institutis et Personis* (4. ed., 2 vols., Romae, 1909), II, (62); Piatus Montensis, *Praelectiones Juris Regularis* (3. ed., 2 vols., Tornaci, 1906), I, 115.

[50] S.C. Ep. et Reg., decr. 22 apr. 1796—*AJP,* XVI (1877), 733.

[51] Ojetti, *Synopsis Rerum Moralium et Juris Pontificii* (3. ed., 4 vols., Romae, 1909-1914), "Novitiatus." (Hereafter cited as *Synopsis.*)

[52] Battandier, *Guide canonique pour les constitutions des instituts à voeux simples* (6. ed., Paris, 1923), p. 107, note 1 (hereafter cited as *Guide canonique*); Meynard, *Réponses canoniques et pratiques de religieuses à voeux simples* (2. ed., Paris, 1891), p. 195 (hereafter cited as *Réponses canoniques*); Piatus Montensis, *Praelectiones Juris Regularis,* I, 115; Bastien, *Directoire Canonique a l'usage des Congrégations à voeux simples* (4. ed., Bruges, 1933), pp. 320-322 (hereater cited as *Directoire Canonique*).

PART II
CANONICAL COMMENTARY

CHAPTER III

THE OFFICE OF THE NOVICE MASTER

ARTICLE 1. PRELIMINARY NOTES ON THE APPLICATION OF THE LAW

A. The Mistress of Novices

IN the treatment of the legislation of Canon Law on the Novice Master it must be understood that whatever is said of the Novice Master applies also to the Mistress of Novices in religious Institutes of women, unless, of course, it is clear from either the context or from the nature of the matter treated that only the Master and not the Mistress is included in the law. This is an obvious and necessary deduction from the general principle of canon 490.[1]

Hence, whatever is said of the qualifications required of the Novice Master, or of the nature of his power, for example, will apply also to Mistresses of Novices. On the other hand, when the law treats of the Master as confessor, then, because of the very nature of the case, there obviously can be no application to the Mistress of Novices.

B. Societies Living in Common without Public Vows

There arises the question whether or not the law concerning the Master of Novices is applicable to those Societies, whether of men or of women, whose members live in common after the manner of

[1] "Quae de religiosis statuuntur, etsi masculino vocabulo expressa, valent etiam pari iure de mulieribus, nisi ex contextu sermonis vel ex rei natura aliud constet."

religious but who are not bound by public vows. Such Societies cannot properly be called religious Institutes, nor can the members be called religious in the canonical sense.[2]

Within the canons[3] treating of these Societies there are some explicit stipulations requiring that the law on certain points concerning religious be observed in these Societies as well. However, the general principle established by canon 675 is that such Societies are to be governed according to their own proper constitutions. Therefore it is incorrect to apply the law concerning religious Institutes to these Societies unless the Code expressly commands this in certain instances. In regard to the novitiate and the Novice Master the Code gives no such command aside from that which requires canon 542[4] to be observed in admitting candidates to the novitiate.[5] Therefore, as regards the Novice Master the constitutions proper to each such Society are to be followed. Had the legislator wished the law for religious to be followed, he would have inserted mention of this in the law, as was actually done in the Code's reference to canon 542.

It could be objected that, since there is no express prescription of the law concerning the Novice Master in these Societies, there becomes applicable the principle of canon 20, in accordance with which a norm must be taken from laws established for similar matters —in this case, from the laws governing the Novice Master in religious Institutes.

This objection seems to miss the point at issue. For, before this principle of canon 20 may be applied, there must be a lacuna in the general and particular law regarding some definite point, as canon 20 itself states. In this case there is no such lacuna, for the law, as expressed in canon 675, supposes that such Societies have their own particular law governing the novitiate and the Novice Master.

[2] Cf. canons 675, § 1; 488, 1° and 7°.

[3] Canons 673-681.

[4] This canon is concerned with impediments to entrance into the novitiate.

[5] Canon 677.

Hence it is wrong to apply the law concerning the Novice Master to these Societies in virtue of the designated principle as enunciated in canon 20.[6]

In support of the opinion that these Societies are not bound by the law governing the novitiate, Goyeneche cites a declaration of the Pontifical Commission for the Authentic Interpretation of the Code.[7] The Commission was asked whether certain canons concerning ecclesiastical penalties were applicable to clerical Societies which were not religious Institutes in the legal sense. Among the canons listed by the questioner was canon 2411, which is concerned with the penalties to which religious Superiors are liable for contravening the prescriptions of canons 542, 544 and 571, § 2. The first two of these canons, in turn, treat of certain requisites for admission into the novitiate, and the last one treats of admission to religious profession. The Commission answered that the first part of canon 2411 did apply to such Societies, while as to the rest of the canon there was to be no derogation from the constitutions of the Society.

Apparently the Commission answered in this fashion because the general law itself in canon 677 requires that these Societies observe canon 542, while on the other hand the law makes no mention whatever of canon 544 and 571, § 2, thereby leaving the determination of these points of law to the constitutions of the individual Societies concerned. In other words, the response of the Pontifical Commission was tantamount to saying that the penalties established by the second part of canon 2411 do not apply to these Societies for the obvious reason that the general law does not require these Societies to observe canons 544 and 571, § 2.

At first blush this contention, and indeed the very response of the Pontifical Commission may seem to contradict the principle of canon 2219, § 3, which forbids the application of canonical penalties from one case to another in view simply of an analogous status. But,

[6] Cf. Goyeneche, "Consultatio"—*Commentarium pro Religiosis* (later 1935 *Commentarium pro Religiosis et Missionariis*, Romae, 1920—), IV (1923), 340-341, where this same argument is proposed. (Hereafter this periodical will be cited as *CpR* and *CpRM* respectively.)

[7] 2-3 June, 1918—*Acta Apostolicae Sedis, Commentarium Officiale* (Romae, 1909-1929; Civitate Vaticana, 1929—), X (1918) 347 (hereafter cited as *AAS*).

as Maroto (1875-1937) pointed out,[8] this is not an instance of applying the penalty to a case not considered by the law itself. Rather, it is a mere declaration stating that the penalty in question does apply to clerical Societies, not by analogy but in virtue of the general law itself. For canon 2411 is applicable to all transgressors of the penal laws mentioned in canon 2411. Hence all those who are bound by these laws are subject to the penalties threatened by canon 2411.

Now, since the law itself in canon 677 states that these Societies are required to observe the law of canon 542, the Pontifical Commission declared that the penalties threatened against religious Superiors who transgress the law of canon 542 likewise apply to these Societies. Conversely, it seems evident that the reason why the Commission declared that the second part of canon 2411 did not apply to these Societies was not because of the principle forbidding the application of penalties from case to case in view of any existing analogy, but rather for the more fundamental reason that the law to which the penalty is attached did not apply to these Societies. If canons 544 and 571, § 2, did apply to these Societies, why should the Commission have said that the penalties attached to these laws do not apply, when it had just stated that in the case of canon 542, which certainly is binding for these Societies, the penalty did apply? Hence it seems perfectly logical to cite this decision of the Pontifical Commission in support of the contention that the law concerning the Novice Master does not apply to Societies whose members live in common without public vows.[9]

Article 2. Nature of the Office

The office of the Novice Master cannot be called an ecclesiastical office in the strict sense of the term, for neither the power of orders nor that of jurisdiction is attached to it as such. However, it is an ecclesiastical office in the wide sense, since it is legitimately exercised for a spiritual end.[10] The nature of the office consists in this

[8] "Annotationes"—*CpR,* I (1920), 106.

[9] Cf. Schaefer, *De Religiosis ad Normam Codicis Iuris Canonici* (3. ed., Romae: S.A.L.E.R., 1940), p. 1032 (hereafter cited as *De Religiosis*); Goyeneche, *art. cit., loc. cit.*); Maroto, *art. cit.,* p. 107.

[10] Cf. canon 145.

that the Novice Master is the superior of the novices [11] and as their superior is charged with their formation and instruction in everything pertaining to the religious state. Just what is included under this will be considered in Chapter VI.

Article 3. Necessity of the Office

The law states that a Novice Master must be placed in charge of the novices.[12] The Constitution *Cum ad regularem* clearly seems to imply that religious Superiors have a grave obligation to appoint a Novice Master over the novices.[13] Several authors, commenting on the present law of the Code, hold that this is undoubtedly a grave obligation.[14] This is clear since canon 559, § 1, and the very nature of the novitiate demand a Novice Master. For both the instruction and the formation of the novices as well as their probation by the religious Institute require that some superior be officially in charge of them. Hence religious Superiors who would be delinquent in appointing a Novice Master would undoubtedly be guilty objectively of grave sin.[15]

Though it is required by law—and hence required for the lawfulness of the novitiate—that there be a Novice Master, there arises the question whether the Master is so necessary to the novitiate that, unless one is put in charge of it, or unless some other religious acts as his vicar during the year of probation, the novitiate would be invalid. Schaefer is of the opinion that, should the Master or a

[11] Cf. Vermeersch-Creusen, *Epitome Iuris Canonici* (3. ed., 3 vols., Mechliniae-Romae: Dessain, 1927-1928), I, n. 663. (Hereafter cited as *Epitome.*)

[12] Canon 559, § 1.

[13] Clemens VIII, const. *"Cum ad regularem,"* 19 mart. 1603, §§ 2, 15—*Fontes,* n. 189.

[14] Schaefer, *De Religiosis,* p. 529; Larraona, "Commentarium Codicis"—*CpRM,* XXIII (1942), 253; Goyeneche, "Consultatio"—*CpRM,* XVIII (1937), 158; Berutti, *Institutiones Iuris Canonici* (6 vols., Vol. III, *De Religiosis,* Taurini-Romae: Marietti, 1936), III, 178. (Hereafter cited as *De Religiosis.*)

[15] Cf. Goyeneche, "Consultatio"—*CpRM,* XVIII (1937), 157-158.

legitimate substitute be absent throughout the year, the novitiate would certainly be illicit, but not invalid.[16] Berutti is of the same opinion.[17]

However, some commentators[18] maintain that the Master is required for the validity of the novitiate as well as for its lawfulness. Larraona[19] maintains that, although there is no clear place in the law where it is expressly stated that the Novice Master is necessary for the validity of the novitiate, nevertheless it seems sufficiently clear that this is stated equivalently.[20] He argues that the Novice Master is so essential to the novitiate that he can rightly be called the Superior of the novitiate to the extent that its government belongs exclusively to him alone. Moreover, since the instruction, formation and probation of the novices evidently are substantial elements of the novitiate,[21] they demand the presence of a Novice Master if they are to be properly achieved. Besides, he continues, these necessary elements of the novitiate completely exclude the possibility for the novices to train and form themselves. Larraona clearly summarizes his opinion by stating (1) that without the designation and at least the habitual presence of a Master the novitiate is invalid; (2) that he who takes the place of the Master, or supplies for him when he is legitimately impeded or absent, must himself be regarded a Novice Master; (3) that the continual presence of the Master is not required for the validity of the novitiate, nor do the various absences of the Master affect its validity, provided that his place is supplied by another, or the absences themselves do not destroy that habitual presence which the Code supposes as an essential requisite of the novitiate.

From Larraona's argumentation it seems a fair and logical conclusion to say that, in his view, the law regarding the designation of a Novice Master and his habitual presence in the novitiate fulfills with

[16] *De Religiosis*, p. 529.

[17] *De Religiosis*, p. 178.

[18] Vito, *De Religiosis* (Napoli: Pontificia Facoltà Giuridica di Napoli, 1943), p. 203; Larraona, "Commentarium Codicis"—*CpRM*, XXIII (1942), 253-254.

[19] *Art. cit., loc. cit.*

[20] Cf. canon 11.

[21] Cf. canons 562; 563; 565.

sufficient clarity the requirements of the term *"aequivalenter"* of canon 11. Thus, according to Larraona's view, canon 559, § 1, is an invalidating law affecting the validity of the novitiate itself.

This position does not seem correct. For although the authors are by no means in complete agreement as to the correct meaning of the term *"aequivalenter"* of canon 11, still many noteworthy canonists [22] interpret *"aequivalenter"* to signify 'words meaning the same thing,' that is, words which are equal to an express declaration of nullity.[23] Both the express and the equivalent phrase can declare an act invalid either explicitly or implicitly.[24] The phrase *"excardinatio . . . effectum non sortitur nisi . . ."* of canon 116 is an example of a phrase which equivalently, though explicitly, declares an act invalid. Canon 39, on the other hand, equivalently but implicitly declares favors granted by a rescript to be invalid if the rescript itself establishes any essential conditions for the granting of the favor and these are not fulfilled.

Now, neither in the law regarding the Novice Master, nor in the comprehensively enumerated list of conditions for a valid novitiate,[25] is there used any phrase or terminology which can be construed as stating equivalently that without the designation or the habitual presence of the Novice Master the novitiate itself is invalid. Larraona's opinion seems to rest on the fact that he considers the office and the duties of the Novice Master [26] of such importance for prop-

[22] Van Hove, *De Legibus Ecclesiasticis* (Mechliniae-Romae: Dessain, 1930), p. 168; Michiels, *Normae Generales Juris Canonici* (2 vols., Lublin: Universitas Catholica, 1929), I, 275-277 (hereafter cited as *Normae Generales*); Vermeersch-Creusen, *Epitome*, I, n. 76; Wernz-Vidal, *Ius Canonicum* (7 vols. in 8, Romae: Universitas Gregoriana, 1923-1938), I, n. 163, note 145; Cicognani, *Canon Law* (Philadelphia: Dolphin Press, 1934), p. 562; Beste, *Introductio in Codicem* (2. ed., Collegeville, Minn.: St. John's Abbey Press, 1944), p. 67; Toso, *Ad Codicem Juris Canonici Commentaria Minora* (5 vols. in 2, Romae: Marietti, 1921-1927), I, 36 (hereafter cited as *Commentaria Minora*).

[23] Van Hove, *De Legibus Ecclesiasticis*, p. 168.

[24] Cf. Michiels, *Normae Generales*, I, 275-276.

[25] Cf. Goyeneche, "Consultatio"—*CpRM*, XX (1939), 310-311.

[26] Cf. canons 561, § 1; 562; 563; 565.

erly achieving the purpose of the novitiate that he deduces the stipulation of canon 559, § 1,[27] to be a necessary condition for the validity of the novitiate.

The importance and necessity of the Novice Master cannot be denied. Indeed, his designation and habitual residence may even be regarded a form or solemnity necessary for the novitiate. But not every law prescribing such a form or solemnity thereby nullifies an act (in this case the novitiate) lacking the prescribed form. The nullifying effect itself must be established in the law by means of a distinct and personal act of the legislator's will.[28] To determine whether or not this invalidating effect has actually been established, one must have recourse not only to the ruling contained in canon 11, but also to the ruling incorporated in canon 18, which delineates the principles according to which the meaning of the law is to receive its proper interpretation.

Now, according to the principles of canon 18, ecclesiastical laws must first of all be understood according to the proper meaning of the words of the law considered in their text and context. In the text and context of the law on the Novice Master there is nothing which *directly* indicates that the Master is required for the validity of the novitiate. Nor does it seem correct to say that the law on the Novice Master is obscure and doubtful, and accordingly to have recourse to the principles established by the second part of canon 18 for the interpretation of doubtful passages of the law.

Hence to make the *deduction* that, because of the importance and necessity of the Novice Master, his designation and habitual presence equivalently condition the validity of the novitiate seems to be straining the legal aspects of the question. For such a conclusion is arrived at only *indirectly* through a rationalization, rather than through a legal interpretation of the proper meaning of the words of the law.

The point to be established is: does the *law* equivalently say *in*

[27] "Novitiorum institutioni praeficiendus est Magister. . . ."

[28] Michiels, *Normae Generales,* I, 275; canon 1680, § 1: Nullitas actus tunc tantum habetur, cum in eo deficiunt quae actum ipsum essentialiter constituunt, aut sollemnia seu conditiones desiderantur a sacris canonibus requisitae sub poena nullitatis.

any given phrase that, unless a Novice Master is designated and unless he is habitually present, the novitiate is invalid. The present writer cannot agree that it does. For the term *aequivalenter* of canon 11 certainly appears to mean *in equivalent terminology,* and not *through an equivalent rationalization or deduction.*

The presumption of law is that no law is an invalidating one unless the contrary is expressly or equivalently stated.[29] True, canon 559, § 1 explicitly states that a Master must be designated. Likewise it implicitly states that he, or a legitimate substitute, must reside habitually in the novitiate.[30] Certainly this is sufficient to oblige the Master to habitual residence. But it is not sufficient to justify the conclusion that his presence is therefore required for the validity of the novitiate. This itself must be stated in the law at least equivalently, either explicitly or implicitly.[31]

Larraona rightly says that the instruction, exercise and probation of the novices are essential elements of the novitiate.[32] These elements, he continues, demand a Novice Master, whose task it is to instruct and form the novices, and, secondly, these elements exclude the possibility of the novices autonomously instructing and forming themselves. Hence, since this scope of the novitiate cannot be achieved without a Novice Master, Larraona concludes that the Master is essential for a valid novitiate. In other words, he seems to be arguing from the end or purpose of the law which requires a Novice Master that the Master is essential for a valid novitiate.

A similar argument is proposed by Prikryl.[33] This author considers a case wherein the Novice Master was absent from the novitiate for eight months, returning only two months before the time set for the profession of the novices. During his absence no other religious, not even a *Socius,* had been appointed to take his place. The author

[29] Canon 11; cf. Michiels, *Normae Generales,* I, 275.

[30] Cf. canons 559, § 1; 561, § 1; 562; 565, § 1. The Constitution *Cum ad regularem* in § 8 explicitly stated that the Master was to reside within the cloister proper to the novices.—*Fontes,* n. 189.

[31] Michiels, *Normae Generales,* I, 275; cf. Goyeneche, "Consultatio"—*CpRM,* XVIII (1937), 157-158.

[32] "Commentarium Codicis"—*CpRM,* XXIII (1942), 254.

[33] "Ein sonderbares Noviziat"—*Theologisch-praktische Quartalschrift* (Linz, 1832—), XCI (1938), 112-116. (Hereafter this periodical will be cited as *TPQ.*)

is rather reluctant to pass a final judgment on the question of such a novitiate's validity. Yet he does say it is his belief that, if the case had been submitted to the Sacred Congregation of Religious, the latter would not have granted either a *sanatio* of that year of novitiate, or a dispensation from the obligation of repeating it. His reason for this opinion is that the purpose of the novitiate was not achieved. Therefore, he clearly seems to imply that in his opinion the year of novitiate in question was invalid.

To the present writer, the position of these authors does not seem a justifiable one. For the end and purpose of a law does not of itself intrinsically determine the extent and scope of the law. Rather, it is the will of the legislator as expressed in the verbal formula of the law that determines its nature and extent. Hence, *per se* and directly, there can be said to have been willed by the legislator only those things which he has expressed in the words of his law. The words of the law in turn, according to the principles of canon 18, must be interpreted according to their proper meaning considered in their text and context. When the meaning is sufficiently clear, it is not only unnecessary but also absolutely contrary to the nature of law to interpret the law further on other principles. Hence, when the meaning of the words of the law is sufficiently clear, an interpretation which neglects the verbal formula of the law, or treats it only secondarily, and instead attempts to determine the will of the legislator solely by considering the end and purpose of the law, must be absolutely rejected.[34] Hence, to argue that the Novice Master is an essential requisite of a valid novitiate because of the purpose of the law which requires the Master seems to be an improper interpretation of the wording of the law.

The proper conclusion, therefore, at least in this writer's opinion, seems to be that the designation and habitual residence of the Novice Master are not required for the validity of the novitiate. Even should it be argued that it is doubtful whether or not this is an invalidating law,[35] it would still follow that the law would not

34 Michiels, *Normae Generales,* I, 421-422.

35 Goyeneche, though apparently holding that the Master is not required for the validity of the novitiate, seems to imply that the law might be called doubtful.—"Consultatio"—*CpRM,* XVIII (1937), 157-158.

bind with invalidating effect until it has clearly been shown to be a certainly invalidating law.[36]

A supplementary argument might be drawn from the fact that, if the Novice Master were required for the validity of the novitiate, the novices concerned would seem to be unduly penalized and barred from profession because of the malfeasance of the superiors in neglecting to appoint a Novice Master, or of the Novice Master himself in neglecting to reside habitually in the novitiate.[37]

The strongest objection, it would seem, that might be advanced against the position defended here would be the following. Since the present law requiring a Novice Master is derived entirely from legislation enacted before the promulgation of the Code, it follows that it must be understood as was the older law, and interpreted in the same way as the approved authors interpreted the former legislation.[38] Hence if it can be shown that the older legislation was interpreted as requiring the Novice Master for the validity of the novitiate, this same interpretation must be put upon the present law.

Having investigated a considerble number of the more important older commentators, the writer has come to the following conclusions. The commentators unanimously maintained that since the Council of Trent [39] a full year of probation was a necessary requisite for a valid profession of vows. Likewise all considered whether or not this probation had to last for a complete year *de momento ad momentum,* whether or not the wearing of the religious habit was required for the validity of the novitiate, and other such questions. However, not all the authors were in agreement in their conclusions about these points.[40] But among all these commentators there could

[36] Cf. canon 15: Leges, etiam irritantes et inhabilitantes, in dubio iuris non urgent. On the meaning of this law cf. Michiels, *Normae Generales,* I, 334.

[37] Cf. Reg. 22, R.J., in VI°:—Non debet aliquis alterius odio praegravari.

[38] Cf. canon 6, 2°.

[39] Cf. Sess. XXV, *de regularibus,* c. 15.

[40] Cf. Reiffenstuel, *Jus Canonicum Universum* (5 vols. in 3, Venetiis, 1760), lib. III, tit. XXXI, nn. 92, 94, 103-108; Schmalzgrueber, *Jus Ecclesiasticum Universum* (5 vols. in 3, Neapoli, 1738), lib. III, tit. XXXI, nn. 56-59; Suarez, *Opera Omnia* (28 vols., Parisiis, 1856-1878, Vols. XV-XVI, *De Religione,* 1859-

be found only two who went any further in their investigation of the essence of a valid probation.

Suarez (1548-1617), in investigating what constituted the essence of a valid novitiate, maintained that it was altogether necessary to distinguish between the state of probation and actual probation.[41] Wernz (1842-1914) also made this same distinction.[42]

The state of probation, according to these authors, consisted in this that the novice was present in a house legitimately designated as a place of probation, so that he and the religious Institute might be able to examine and test each other. The actual probation of the novice was accomplished through the exercises and activities of the novitiate.

The state of probation, therefore, had two essential elements: one negative and the other positive. The negative element consisted in the fact that the novice had not yet made a profession of vows in the religious Institute in which he was a novice. This was essential, since the state of probation was terminated by the act of profession. The positive element, on the other hand, consisted, not in the particular acts of probation usually experienced in the novitiate, but rather in the novice's voluntary continuance in the state of probation. This, in turn, was manifested by the novice through some external sign as, for instance, the wearing of the religious habit. The Institute manifested its agreement to this continuance of the novice in the state of probation by accepting the novice's manifestation of his will to remain. As a result of this the Institute was enabled to examine the qualities of the novice, and the novice himself was prepared to submit to actual probation.[43]

Suarez explicitly stated that no actual probation except this voluntary continuance in the state of probation was of the essence

1860), tract. VII, lib. V, cap. XII-XV (hereafter cited as *De Religione*); *Salmanticensis Collegii Cursus Theologiae Moralis* (6 vols. in 4, Vols. I-II, 6. ed., 1722; Vols. III-IV, ed. novissima, 1714; Vol. V, 1725; Vol. VI, 1724, Venetiis), tom. IV, tract. XV, cap. III, nn. 1-32. (Hereafter cited as *Salmanticenses.*)

41 *De Religione,* tract. VII, lib. V, cap. XIV, n. 3.

42 *Ius Decretalium,* III, n. 634.

43 Suarez, *op. cit.*, nn. 4, 7, 8; Wernz, *loc. cit.*; cf. Wernz-Vidal, *Ius Canonicum,* III, n. 275 where the same opinion is proposed.

of the novitiate.[44] As long as the novice persevered in this state, even though he was not subjected to any actual probation by the Institute, the novitiate was valid. The Superiors, of course, were at fault, but the novice was not to be debarred from profession on this account, since actual probation was not essential for a valid novitiate.

If one adopt the opinion of these two authors, it seems logical to conclude that, since actual probation of the novices was not essential to a valid novitiate, neither was the designation and the habitual residence of the Novice Master essential. For the whole purpose of his presence in the novitiate was to be the moderator of the probation and formation of the novices.[45] Hence, it can be said that, though few of the authors in the interpretation of the law prior to the Code treated the precise point, their interpretation clearly favored the opinion that the Novice Master was not regarded necessary for a valid novitiate.

A final question arises here as to the number of Novice Masters in the one novitiate. The Code apparently supposes that the entire group of novices will be under the care of one Master, even though the group consist of two distinct classes of novices, choir and lay novices. Still there seems to be no reason in law why there cannot be a distinct novitiate house and a separate Master for the lay novices apart from the house that has been established and the Master who has been appointed for the choir novices.[46]

Nor does it seem to be forbidden to have a separate Master for each of the two classes of novices, both classes however living in the one house of novitiate.[47] Such a division might be thought feasible, for example, because of the large number of the novices. But in cases wherein this latter division exists, the novitiate, as is implied in canon 554, §§ 1 and 2, would remain a juridic unit.[48] Hence, in

[44] *De Religione,* tract. VII, lib. V, cap. XIV, n. 8.

[45] Cf. canons 561-563; 565, which now, as then, indicate the purpose of the Novice Master's presence among the novices.

[46] Cf. canon 558.

[47] Schaefer, *De Religiosis,* pp. 530; 534.

[48] Wernz-Vidal, *Ius Canonicum,* III, n. 283, note 29; Schaefer, *De Religiosis,* p. 534; Goyeneche, "Consultatio"—*CpR,* VIII (1927), 116-117; *CpRM,* XXIII (1942), 265-267.

Institutes of pontifical approval no special Apostolic Indult would be necessary for such a division of the novitiate, supposed, of course, that the permission of the Holy See had already been obtained for the erection of the novitiate.[49]

It must be noted however that in cases wherein such a division exists each Master would have complete charge of the government of the class of novices in his care. The one Novice Master could not interfere with the instruction and formation of the other Master's charges. The novices in turn would be subject only to that Master who is placed over them.[50]

Though apparently there is nothing in law to forbid such a division of the novitiate, nevertheless it seems to be contrary to the intention of the law. For both the Clementine Constitution [51] and the Code of Canon Law suppose that all the novices of one province, if the Institute is so divided, will be trained in one novitiate house under one and the same Novice Master.[52] Moreover, the Code itself provides for an assistant or *Socius* to be assigned to the Novice Master to aid him in the government of the novitiate.[53] Furthermore, it requires that the lay novices have their own separate section of the novitiate house, that special instructions in Christian doctrine be given to them, and legislates as to what domestic duties may be performed by them during the time of probation.[54] But all these points of law are based on the supposition that the lay novices are dwelling in the same novitiate house and are in the care of the same

[49] Cf. canon 554, §§ 1, 2; Goyeneche, "Consultatio"—*CpR*, VIII (1927), 117.

[50] Canon 561, §§ 1, 2.

[51] Clemens VIII, const. *"Cum ad regularem,"* 19 mart. 1603, §§ 8, 9, 15—*Fontes*, n. 189.

[52] Berutti, *De Religiosis*, p. 180. In monasteries of *moniales* in which there are extern sisters, all the novices are to be trained by one Mistress of Novices, according to the norms of the Sacred Congregation of Religious as issued on July 16, 1931, art. 31, 32, 34.—cf. *Apollinaris* (Romae, 1928—), IV (1931), 349.

[53] Canon 559, § 2.

[54] Canons 564, § 2; 565, §§ 2, 3.

Master of Novices as are the choir novices.[55] Finally, Vermeersch-Creusen mention that the Sacred Congregation of Religious is not accustomed to allow two Novice Masters in the same novitiate.[56]

Article 4. Qualifications Required

The qualifications required of the Novice Master were first expressed in law by Clement VIII (1592-1605).[57] According to the Clementine law the Novice Master was required to be a priest,[58] at least thirty-five years of age, and ten years professed. He was likewise to be of such character and virtue as to be a model for those whom he was to direct.[59] These qualities became the norm thereafter, and the constitutions of the various religious Institutes developed them profusely.[60]

In his Constitution *Sanctissimus*, Innocent XII (1691-1700) renewed these prescriptions of Clement VIII and commanded religious Superiors to assign to the house of the novitiate only such religious as were staid and exemplary in character, given to prayer and mortification, and zealous for the regular observance and the purity of the rule. These religious were to be outstanding in thoughtfulness and charity toward those under their care, providing for them even in their temporal necessities, and being especially devoted to the sick. Moreover, the Pope warned Superiors that if they were negligent, and much more if they were found contumacious in dis-

[55] Cf. Goyeneche, "Consultatio"—*CpR*, VIII (1927), 116.

[56] *Epitome*, I, n. 663. Perhaps these authors meant to indicate the mind of the Sacred Congregation on this matter. For otherwise it would appear to be a somewhat strange statement in the light of the fact that no special permission seems to be required to have a separate Novice Master for each of the two classes of novices.

[57] Clemens VIII, const. *"Cum ad regularem,"* 19 mart. 1603—*Fontes*, n. 189.

[58] This was required because, as already stated, the Constitution *Cum ad regularem* originally applied only to regulars. When the norms of this Constitution were adapted for other Institutes the requirement that the Master be a priest was necessary only in clerical Institutes.—Cf. Battandier, *Guide canonique*, p. 407, note 1.

[59] Clemens VIII, const. *"Cum ad regularem,"* 19 mart. 1603, § 9—*Fontes*, n. 189.

[60] Battandier, *Guide canonique*, p. 410.

regard of this matter of assigning only exemplary religious to the house of the novitiate, they would be subject to grave penalties. Such Superiors were liable not only to the privation of any office they held, but also to the perpetual ineligibility to be reappointed to such an office or to any others.[61]

The present law of the Code is substantially identical with that of Clement VIII. Canon 559, § 1, requires that the Novice Master be (1) at least thirty-five years of age; (2) at least ten years professed, the years being reckoned from the time of his first profession; (3) outstanding for his prudence, charity, piety and religious observance; and, (4) in a clerical Institute, ordained to the priesthood. Each of these qualifications will be examined in turn.

A. Age

The Novice Master must be at least thirty-five years of age.[62] Since the law requires this as a minimum, the particular rules and constitutions of an Institute could legitimately demand a more advanced age.

The Code does not explicitly state that the thirty-five years must be completed. However, it seems clearly implied that they must be, and this according to the norm of canon 34, § 3, 3°. For the very wording of the law (*"annos natus"*) seem to mean that he must have been born for thirty-five years. Unless a person has completed his thirty-fifth year he cannot rightly be said to have been born for thirty-five years. This seems to be the common teaching of most of the canonists.[63]

[61] Innocentius XII, const. *"Sanctissimus,"* 18 iul. 1695—*Bullarium Ordinis FF. Praedicatorum* (8 vols., Romae, 1729-1740), VI, 414-415.

[62] Canon 559, § 1.—The Code, in canon 504, requires that the major Superiors, the Superior General excluded, be only thirty years of age. The more advanced age required in the case of the Novice Master may be regarded as an indication that the law demands greater experience for this important office.

[63] Cf. Schaefer, *De Religiosis*, p. 530; Coronata, *Institutiones Iuris Canonici* (5 vols., Vols. I-II, 2. ed., Taurini: Marietti, 1933-1939), I, n. 585, note 7 (hereafter cited *Institutiones*); De Meester, *Juris Canonici et Juris Canonico-Civilis Compendium* (ed. nova, 3 vols. in 4, Brugis: Desclée, 1921-1928), II, 440, note 5 (hereafter cited *Compendium J.C.*); Fanfani, *De Iure Religiosorum*

It may be asked whether the attainment of the age required of the Novice Master is necessary for the valid appointment to the office, and even for the validity of the novitiate itself and the subsequent profession of the novices. It seems clearly correct to say that this is not a requirement for the valid appointment of the Novice Master. The Code does not mention it as a condition for validity; nor can it be inferred to be such from the principles of canon 11. Moreover, as Goyeneche points out,[64] if the age of the Novice Master is required for the validity of the appointment to the office, then it must likewise be said that the other qualities required by canon 559, § 1, are also necessary for its validity. Goyeneche does not hesitate to say that no one holds such an opinion.

Without a proper dispensation, the nomination of a religious of less than a full thirty-five years of age as Novice Master would be unlawful, but not invalid. Much less would the novitiate and the subsequent profession of the novices be invalid. For if, as has already been shown, the Novice Master himself is not necessary for the validity of the novitiate, much less would the required age be necessary for it.

A Novice Master who does not possess the required age should either be removed from office, or a dispensation should be sought from the Holy See. According to Goyeneche[65] the Holy See is accustomed to dispense quite readily as far as the age of the Novice Master is concerned. In regard to diocesan Institutes it should be noted that, as a general principle, the Bishop is not empowered to grant a dispensation in this matter.[66]

B. Profession

It is likewise necessary that the Novice Master be a religious who has been professed at least ten years.[67] As with the age re-

(2. ed., Taurini-Romae: Marietti, 1925), n. 206; Larraona, "Commentarium Codicis"—*CpRM*, XXIII (1942), 255; Goyeneche, "Consultatio"—*CpR*, VI (1925), 487-488.

[64] "Consultatio"—*CpRM*, XX (1939), 310; Vito, *De Religiosis*, p. 204.

[65] *Art. cit.*, *ibid.*, p. 311.

[66] Cf. canon 81.

[67] Canon 559, § 1.

quirement, the Code leaves room for the possibility of a longer time of profession being required by individual rules and constitutions. These years are to be computed from the first profession of vows, that is, from that profession which is made at the end of the novitiate. These years too must be completed according the norm of canon 34, § 3, 3°.[68]

The Code does not state expressly that the profession must have been made in the same religious Institute in which the religious is appointed Novice Master. Such a requirement is demanded in the case of major Superiors.[69] But because of the difference of the wording in canons 504 and 559, § 1, Creusen ventures the opinion that the ten years of profession need not be in the one institute.[70]

He envisions the case of a religious who has transferred from one Institute to another after having been professed for several years in the first Institute. It would be an exceptional case, Creusen admits, but not an altogether imaginary one for such a religious sufficiently to acquire the spirit of his new Institute within a short time to such a degree that he could be appointed Novice Master, provided that the sum total of his years as a professed religious in both Institutes amount to at least ten complete years.

It might well be true that such a religious could acquire the spirit of his new Institute in a brief time. But the point to be established is: is this the meaning of the law? Berutti [71] and Larraona [72] disagree with this opinion, and apparently rightly so. For although neither the constitution *Cum ad regularem* [73] nor canon 559, § 1, states it expressly (and thereby leaves some room for doubt), still practically all the authors interpret the law as requiring ten years

68 De Meester, *Compendium J.C.*, II, 440, note 5; Berutti, *De Religiosis*, p. 180; Schaefer, *De Religiosis*, p. 530.

69 Cf. canon 504.

70 Creusen-Garesché-Ellis, *Religious Men and Women in the Code* (3. ed., Milwaukee: Bruce, 1940), p. 154. Cf. Bastien, *Directoire Canonique*, p. 323, where this same opinion is proposed.

71 *De Religiosis*, p. 180.

72 "Commentarium Codicis"—*CpRM*, XXIII (1942), 255-256, note 1072.

73 Clemens VIII, const. *"Cum ad regularem,"* 19 mart. 1603, § 9—*Fontes*, n. 189.

of profession in the one Institute.[74] The reason for this interpretation is that the constitution *Cum ad regularem* was understood in no other way by the commentators.[75] Hence, since the Code adopted the law of this Constitution, it is to be interpreted in the same way as the older law was interpreted by the older commentators.[76] Moreover, Larraona [77] argues that, if profession in the same Institute is demanded of the major Superiors, there is all the more reason why it should be required also for the Novice Master.

A final question pertaining to the qualification of profession may be raised. In religious Institutes whose members take perpetual vows, must the Novice Master be perpetually professed? The Code does not explicitly treat this, but it seems to be required implicitly by the law. This follows from the fact that the time of temporary profession cannot be prorogued longer than six complete years.[78] Hence, since the Master must be professed at least ten years, it follows that he must also be perpetually professed.

C. *Moral Qualities*

Concerning the moral qualities required in the Novice Master the Code states briefly that he must be conspicuous for his prudence, charity, piety and religious observance.[79] This is substantially what Clement VIII required also.[80] Quoting the passage of the Clementine Constitution, Wernz-Vidal remark that it could hardly be more opportunely or more beautifully expressed.[81] For this reason, and likewise to show what are the implications of the requisites estab-

[74] Cf. Larraona, "Commentarium Codicis"—*CpRM*, XXIII (1942), 255-256, note 1072.

[75] Berutti, *De Religiosis*, p. 180.

[76] Cf. canon 6, 2°.

[77] *Art. cit., loc. cit.*

[78] Canon 574, §§ 1, 2.

[79] Canon 559, § 1.

[80] Clemens VIII, const. *"Cum ad regularem,"* 19 mart. 1603, § 9—*Fontes*, n. 189.

[81] *Ius Canonicum*, III, n. 283, note 29.

lished by the Code, it will not be amiss to quote the passage here. Speaking of the appointment of both the Master and his *Socius*, Clement VIII wrote:

> Let the Superiors be diligently careful that both be outstanding, as far as is possible, in doctrine and in the example of their past lives, given to prayer and to mortification, abounding in prudence and in charity. Let them be sedate, but affable, meek, but zealous for the things of God, free of all disturbance of heart and mind, but especially free from anger and indignation, which usually impede and are alien to charity both in themselves and toward others. Finally, let them be such religious as to be in all things living examples of good, so that those who are committed to their care may not so much fear as revere them, and so that the novices may never be able to malign them.[82]

Though but few of the authors consulted mention it, yet from the law itself and from the very nature and importance of the office, it seems that the Superiors have a serious obligation of appointing a competent religious as Novice Master. Berutti declares that the common law undoubtedly imposes on the Superiors a grave obligation of appointing as Novice Master only a fit religious.[83] Other authors speak of the office as "a most grave duty" [84] and "a grave office," [85] indicating thereby the care and diligence which should be exercised by Superiors in choosing a Master. Among the older authors,

[82] Translation: the writer's. Clemens VIII, const. *"Cum ad regularem,"* 19 mart. 1603, § 9: "Sintque ambo doctrina, et quantum per Superiorum diligentiam, et curam fieri poterit, vitae etiam anteactae exemplo praestantes, Orationis praeterea et mortificationis operibus addicti, prudentia, charitateque referti, non sine affabilitate graves, zelum Dei cum mansuetudine praeseferentes, ab omni cordis, ac animi perturbatione, ira praesertim, et indignatione, quae in se, et erga alios charitatem impedire consueverunt, quam longissime alieni, et tales demum, qui in omnibus seipsos bonorum operum exemplum praebeant, ut ii, qui eorum curae subsunt, illos non tam metuant, quam revereantur, nec illis unquam detrahere quicquam possint."—*Fontes*, n. 189. Quoting this passage Berutti remarks that it is still valid and applicable to the Novice Master because of the very nature of his office.—*De Religiosis*, p. 180.

[83] *De Religiosis*, p. 178.

[84] Pejška, *Ius Canonicum Religiosorum* (3. ed., Friburgi Brisgoviae: Herder, 1927), p. 95.

[85] Schaefer, *De Religiosis*, p. 529.

Reiffenstuel (1642-1703) maintained that only the best qualified and the most outstanding religious were to be deputed as Masters of Novices, since practically the whole welfare of the religious Institute depended upon the formation of the novices. There was little doubt, he added, that those Superiors who were negligent or perfunctory in their selection of Novice Masters, or who appointed an obviously inexperienced young man, or a little qualified older one, omitting to take serious and exact care that they have the necessary qualities, not only did a disservice to their Institute, but likewise were guilty of very grave sin.[86]

D. Priesthood

The final requisite demanded by canon 559, § 1 is that the Novice Master in clerical religious Institutes be a priest. This requirement of the law is clear. However, there arises the question whether or not the Novice Master of those novices who aspire to become lay brothers in a clerical Institute must likewise be a priest. The authors consulted are quite unanimous in saying that he must be a priest.[87] For, since the law itself does not make a distinction, there is no need to distinguish. Moreover, it seems more fitting that the Novice Master over such novices be a priest.

It seems appropriate, too, that the Master in *lay* Institutes of men, some members of which are priests, likewise be a priest. It

[86] *Jus Canonicum Universum,* lib. III, tit. XXXI, n. 91.—"Summa sane cura cuivis Religioni, et media licita adhibenda sunt, ut optime qualificatos, et praestantissimos viros pro Magistris Novitiorum deputet, eo quod a bona educatione Novitiorum, et juventutis Religiosae tota fere salus pendeat Religionum, prout Doctores communiter advertunt, et quotidiana experientia docet, ut proin haud dubie pessime Religioni consulerent, suoque muneri minime satisfacientes gravissime peccarent illi Superiores, qui in selectu horum negligentes, aut perfunctorii existerent, aut obvium quemvis inexpertem juvenem, aut minus qualificatum senem praeficerent, omissa seria et exacta informatione, num debitas pro officio habeat qualitates."

[87] Cf. Schaefer, *De Religiosis,* p. 530; Fanfani, *De Iure Religiosorum,* n. 206; Coronata, *Institutiones,* I, n. 585; Berutti, *De Religiosis,* p. 180; Wernz-Vidal, *Ius Canonicum,* III, n. 283; Vermeersch-Creusen, *Epitome,* I, n. 663; Jansen, *Ordensrecht* (3. ed., Paderborn: Schöningh, 1931), p. 171; Larraona, "Commentarium Codicis"—*CpRM,* XXIII (1942), 257.

must be admitted however that this cannot be urged as an obligation, since the law clearly speaks only of *clerical* Institutes when it requires that the Novice Master be a priest.[88] Yet, even in such lay Institutes the constitutions sometimes reserve the office of Novice Master to its priest members, according to Larraona.[89]

Article 5. Election of the Novice Master

The Clementine legislation required that the Novice Master and his *Socius* be elected by the Provincial Chapter for a period of at least three years. If, outside the time for such a chapter, permission were granted for the erection of a new novitiate house, the Master and his *Socius* could be elected by the Superior General, or the Visitor, with the consent of their council or of other important Fathers. This same procedure was allowed also in case the incumbent Master of Novices died, or if he had to be removed from office.[90]

By these requirements the importance of the office of the Novice Master was manifestly given recognition by the law. It was recognized in the first place that the election to this important office should be given to a chapter and not to one individual. In the extraordinary method of appointment, namely, when one individual was allowed to elect the Master of Novices, not only the counsel of others but their consent as well was required. This required consent was necessary for the validity of the election.[91] Therefore, unless the greater part of the Council consented to the Superior's choice, the election was invalid.[92]

In applying the norms of the Clementine legislation to religious Institutes not bound by the Constitution *Cum ad regularem*, the

[88] Canon 488, 4° defines a clerical Institute as one in which the major portion of the members is promoted to the priesthood.

[89] "Commentarium Codicis"—*CpRM*, XXIII (1942), 257.

[90] Clemens VIII, const. "*Cum ad regularem,*" 19 mart. 1603, § 9—*Fontes*, n. 189.

[91] ". . . quando requiritur consensus Capituli, tenetur Praelatus sequi id, quod major et sanior pars Capitularium concluserit: alioquin nulliter agit."—Reiffenstuel, *Jus Canonicum Universum*, lib. III, tit. X, n. 2.

[92] Cf. *Acta Ordinis Minorum* (Romae, 1882-1886; Florentiae, 1887—), XIX (1900), 206.

Sacred Congregation of Bishops and Regulars employed no hard and fast rule. Consequently the constitutions of the various religious Institutes varied in this regard.[93] Sometimes the Sacred Congregation required that the constitutions of an Institute demand that the Moderatrix General obtain the deliberative vote of her consultors in graver matters, the appointment of the Mistress of Novices being mentioned among these graver matters.[94] At other times it allowed the Superioress General unrestricted discretion in making the appointment of the Mistress of Novices.[95] In the *Normae* of 1901 it was stated that the Moderatrix General together with her council was to elect the Novice Mistress.[96]

Concerning the removal of the Novice Master from office, the various rules differed. Some forbade removal at will, while others required that, if the Master was removed within the period for which he had been elected, the decree of removal had to be approved by the Sacred Congregation.[97]

The *Normae* of 1901 [98] allowed removal, but only for a grave cause, and then only by the Superioress General with the deliberative vote of her council. The *Normae* did not establish any fixed time for the duration of the office.

The Code,[99] departing from the law of the Clementine Constitu-

[93] Battandier, *Guide canonique,* pp. 408-409; Meynard, *Réponses canoniques,* p. 207.

[94] Bizzarri, *Collectanea in usum secretariae Sacrae Congregationis Episcoporum et Regularium* (Romae, 1863), p. 783, ad 5. (Hereafter this collection will be cited as *Collectanea.*)

[95] *AJP,* IX (1867), 388.

[96] *Normae secundum quas S. Congregatio Episcoporum et Regularium procedere solet in Approbandis novis Institutis votorum simplicium,* 28 iun. 1901 (Romae: Typis S.C. de Propaganda Fide, 1901), art. 297. (Hereafter cited as *Normae.*) These *Normae* were not law, but rather a guide for the Sacred Congregation in approving new Institutes whose members professed simple vows. They were concerned chiefly with Institutes of women, but also applied to those of men religious, with the exception of a few articles as noted in the *Normae* themselves. Cf. Vermeersch, *De Religiosis Institutis et Personis* (4. ed., 1909), II, (130), (131).

[97] Cf. Larraona, "Commentarium Codicis"—*CpRM,* XXIV (1943), 26.

[98] Art. 271, 8°.

[99] Canon 560.

tion, states that the Novice Master and his assistant are to be elected according to the form established by the constitutions of each religious Institute. However, it does not necessarily follow that both of them are to be elected in the same manner. The Code certainly allows the possibility of a different form of election for each. The Clementine Constitution, on the contrary, required that the same manner of appointment be followed for both the Novice Master and his *Socius*.[100]

According to Larraona, the constitutions of the various Institutes generally indicate a form of appointment for the Novice Master which differs from that of the appointment of the *Socius*.[101] The constitutions of each Institute must be consulted therefore when one is to determine by whom and in what manner the Master and his *Socius* are to be elected. But in any case it appears to be the mind of the legislator that both the Master and his assistant remain in office for a considerable length of time. They should not be changed too readily, or too often. For, because of the nature of the office, especially that of the Master, experience is of great value, and this can be gained only with time.[102] Still, as Berutti remarks,[103] it is generally not expedient to have as the Novice Master a religious greatly advanced in age. For, as often happens, when one has the same office for many years it becomes likely that he will employ less effort and alacrity in discharging his duties.

In speaking of the appointment of the Novice Master, the Code uses the word *election*. This is not to be taken in the strict canonical sense alone,[104] but also in the wider sense of the word *choose*

[100] Clemens VIII, const. *"Cum ad regularem,"* 19 mart. 1603, § 9—*Fontes*, n. 189.

[101] "Commentarium Codicis"—*CpRM*, XXIV (1943), 26.

[102] Cf. Chelodi-Ciprotti, *Ius Canonicum de Personis* (3. ed., Vincenza: Società Anonima Tipografica, 1942), p. 423, note 3; Coronata, *Institutiones*, I, n. 585; Schaefer, *De Religiosis*, p. 532; Wernz-Vidal, *Ius Canonicum*, III, n. 283; Biederlack-Führich, *De Religiosis* (Oeniponte, 1919), p. 137; Sipos, *Enchiridion Iuris Canonici* (Pécs: Ex Typographia "Haladas R.T.," 1926), p. 353, note 29.

[103] *De Religiosis*, p. 181.

[104] Cf. canons 507; 160-182.

or *nominate*.[105] According to Larraona the more common method today of designating the Novice Master and his *Socius* is by nomination made by the Superior General.[106] To be effective this nomination must have been submitted to a vote of the General Council. This vote, in turn, is deliberative as regards the Master, and consultative as regards the *Socius*.

The Code does not limit the length of time for which the Novice Master and his assistant may hold office. Indeed it explicitly allows re-election. Therefore, should the constitutions of an Institute directly restrict the re-election of the Master or his *Socius*, such a restriction must be accounted contrary to the law of the Code. Hence, according to the principle of canon 489, it would be devoid of legal force and ought to be corrected.[107] But an indirect limitation put on the Novice Master's re-election would not be forbidden. For example, if the constitutions required that the Master be not only at least thirty-five years of age, but also that he be less than sixty. Such a condition might prevent a Novice Master from being re-elected to the office after his term had expired. But this would not be contrary to the law.

If the constitutions fix a definite length of time for the duration of the offices of the Novice Master and his assistant, then removal from office before this term has elapsed demands a just and a grave cause.[108] When the term of office has elapsed, and also if no set time has been fixed by the constitutions, then removal is left to the prudent judgment of the competent Superior. In this case no special cause is required for the removal.[109] Which Superior is the

[105] Cf. Creusen-Garesché-Ellis, *Religious Men and Women in the Code*, p. 154; Schaefer, *De Religiosis*, p. 532; Larraona, "Commentarium Codicis"—*CpRM*, XXIV (1943), 26.

[106] *Art. cit.*, p. 27.

[107] Larraona, "Commentarium Codicis"—*CpRM*, XXIV (1943), 29; Coronata, *Institutiones*, I, n. 585; Vito, *De Religiosis*, p. 205; Blat, *Commentarium Textus Codicis Iuris Canonici* (5 vols. in 6, 1919-1927; Lib. II, *Ius de Religiosis*, 3. ed., 1938, Romae: Apud "Angelicum"), Lib. II, *Ius de Religiosis*, 343 (hereafter cited as *Ius de Religiosis*).

[108] Canon 560.

[109] Cf. Schaefer, *De Religiosis*, p. 532; Beste, *Introductio in Codicem*, p. 375; Vito, *De Religiosis*, p. 205.

competent one in this instance will have to be determined by the constitutions of the Institute. The Code makes no mention of this point.

In those cases wherein the duration of the Master's term of office has been established by the constitutions, his removal without a grave and just cause before the term is finished would indeed be valid, but illicit and juridically unjust. The offended party would have the right to have recourse to the next higher Superior in complaint against the decree of unjust removal from office. The Sacred Congregation of Religious would be the proper body of recourse in those instances wherein the Superior General of the Institute issued the decree of removal.[110]

ARTICLE 6. THE *Socius* TO THE NOVICE MASTER

The Code provides for the appointment of a *Socius* or assistant to the Novice Master to aid him in the government of the novitiate.[111] The Constitution *Cum ad regularem* made a like provision, but the only reason it assigned for the appointment of the *Socius* was the large number of novices.[112] The Code also gives this reason, but goes further by allowing the appointment for any other just cause. Such a cause might be the diversity of language of some of the novices, and the status of health or the advanced age on the part of the Master.[113]

The Code clearly does not contemplate that in every case the Novice Master be given an assistant. However, if, because of the number of the novices or because of some other just reason, it seems to the Superiors concerned that a *Socius* should be appointed, then it seems that they *must* appoint one.[114] But, in any case, it belongs

[110] Cf. Larraona, "Commentarium Codicis"—*CpRM*, XXIV (1943), 29.

[111] Canon 559, § 2.

[112] Clemens VIII, const. *"Cum ad regularem,"* 19 mart. 1603, § 9—*Fontes*, n. 189.

[113] Cf. Berutti, *De Religiosis*, p. 180; Larraona, "Commentarium Codicis"—*CpRM*, XXIII (1942), 257-258.

[114] Berutti, *De Religiosis*, p. 180.

to the Superiors, not to the Novice Master himself, to judge whether or not a *Socius* is to be appointed.[115]

The *Socius* has no proper authority by reason of his office, since the law explicitly states that the government of the novitiate belongs exclusively to the Master.[116] As the assistant to the Novice Master, the *Socius* is subject immediately to him in all things pertaining to the government of the novitiate.[117] Therefore he has only those powers and duties which the Novice Master has committed to him, and these must be exercised and performed under the direction and vigilance of the Master. The *Socius* cannot presume to interfere in any sphere of the government of the novitiate. Otherwise he would be a hindrance rather than a help to the Master.[118]

The form of election of the *Socius,* according to canon 560, is to be determined by the constitutions of each Institute. Therefore, what was said in the previous article[119] anent the election of the Novice Master is applicable likewise to the election of the *Socius.*

The same moral qualifications as required of the Master are required also of the *Socius.*[120] Hence, he must be exemplary in his conduct, outstanding for his piety, prudence, charity and religious observance. However, the *Socius* need be but thirty years of age and five years professed. These years must be complete years computed according to the norms of canon 34, § 3, 3°.[121] The Code requires this age and length of profession as a minimum. Hence the particular constitutions of an Institute could legitimately demand a more advanced age and a longer period of profession.

The Constitution of Clement VIII made no mention at all of profession in regard to the *Socius.* The Code requires that he be at

[115] Schaefer, *De Religiosis,* p. 531; Coronata, *Institutiones,* I, n. 585.

[116] Canon 561, § 1.

[117] Canon 559, § 2.

[118] Cf. Berutti, *De Religiosis,* p. 180; Vermeersch-Creusen, *Epitome,* I, n. 663; Schaefer, *De Religiosis,* p. 532; Larraona, "Commentarium Codicis"—*CpRM,* XXIII (1942), 259.

[119] Chap. III, art. 5.

[120] Canon 559, § 2; Prümmer, *Manuale Iuris Canonici* (5. ed., Friburgi Brisgoviae: Herder, 1927), n. 211.

[121] Schaefer, *De Religiosis,* p. 531; *Coronata, Institutiones,* I, n. 585; Larraona, "Commentarium Codicis"—*CpRM,* XXIII (1942), 259.

least in his sixth year of religious profession, but does not expressly demand that it be perpetual profession. However, according to the general rule of canon 574, § 1, the *Socius* would normally be perpetually professed. Indeed, according to Larraona,[122] the constitutions of the various Institutes usually require that the *Socius* to the Novice Master be perpetually professed. However, if this is not required by the constitutions, it cannot be said that it is a necessary requisite under the general law.

Some authors maintain that the *Socius* to the Novice Master in clerical religious Institutes must be a priest just as the Master himself must be.[123] Schaefer bases his opinion on the fact that the Code requires of the *Socius* the same qualities it demands of the Master.[124] These authors, however, seem to be requiring something that is not demanded by the law. The Code does not state specifically that the *Socius* must have the same qualities as the Novice Master. Rather, having first spoken of the required age and length of profession, it uses the very general phrase: "[and he shall have] the other necessary and fitting qualifications."

It is true that the same moral qualities are required of the *Socius*, since the law must be interpreted in the light of the requisites established by the Clementine Constitution. But as regards the qualification of the priesthood Clement VIII clearly seemed to demand this only of the Novice Master. Immediately after requiring this, the constitution demanded that the Master be thirty-five years old and ten years professed. It then treated of the *Socius* and merely required that he be past thirty years of age. Nothing was mentioned either of profession or of the priesthood. Only after this point did the Clementine Constitution jointly consider the Novice Master and his *Socius* in treating of the required moral qualifications that both had to possess.[125]

122 "Commentarium Codicis"—*CpRM*, XXIII (1942), 260.

123 Schaefer, *De Religiosis*, p. 531; Creusen-Garesché-Ellis, *Religious Men and Women in the Code*, p. 154.

124 Canon 559, § 2: ". . . Magistro novitiorum adiungatur socius . . . cum ceteris dotibus necessariis et opportunis."

125 Clemens VIII, const. *"Cum ad regularem,"* 19 mart. 1603, § 9—*Fontes*, n. 189; cf. *supra* note 82 where the passage on the moral qualities of the Master and his assistant is quoted.

Hence, as several authors point out, the priesthood is not a requisite for the *Socius*.[126] Still, as Vermeersch-Creusen remark,[127] the *Socius* to the Novice Master in clerical religious Institutes usually is a priest. Indeed, the priesthood could be a qualification legitimately required by particular law. When the *Socius* is a priest, he is strictly forbidden to hear the confessions of the novices, unless they themselves freely ask it of him in particular cases and for a grave and urgent reason.[128]

There is nothing in law to forbid the appointment of more than one *Socius* to the Novice Master.[129] The Novice Master could be given more than one assistant when there are large numbers of both choir and lay novices in the novitiate. Yet, it seems that both the Clementine Constitution and the present law of the Code intended that there be but one assistant assigned to aid the Novice Master. And both of these certainly contemplated that the choir and lay novices be trained in one and the same novitiate house.[130] In fact, according to Vermeersch-Creusen, the Sacred Congregation of Religious is not accustomed to allow two *Socii* to be appointed.[131]

Article 7. Incompatible Offices

To guarantee complete freedom to the Novice Master in carrying out his important task, the law of Clement VIII required that both the Novice Master and his *Socius* be free of all other offices and tasks that could hinder them in the care and government of the novices.[132] This general ruling, therefore, left it to jurisprudence

[126] Vermeersch-Creusen, *Epitome,* I, n. 663; Cocchi, *Commentarium in Codicem Iuris Canonici* (8 vols. in 5, Lib. II, *De Personis,* Pars II, Taurinorum Augustae: Marietti, 1924), Lib. II, *De Personis,* Pars II, p. 142 (hereafter cited as *Commentarium*); Larraona, "Commentarium Codicis"—*CpRM,* XXIII (1942), 260.

[127] *Epitome,* I, n. 663.

[128] Canon 891; cf. *infra* Chap. V, art. 2.

[129] Vermeersch-Creusen, *Epitome,* I, n. 663.

[130] Cf. canons 564, § 2; 565, §§ 2, 3; Clemens VIII, const. *"Cum ad regularem,"* 19 mart. 1603, § 9—*Fontes,* n. 189.

[131] *Epitome,* I, n. 663.

[132] Clemens VIII, const. *"Cum ad regularem,"* 19 mart. 1603, § 9—*Fontes,* n. 189.

and to the constitutions of the individual Institutes to determine more specifically just what offices are incompatible with those of the Novice Master and his *Socius*.

The Sacred Congregation of Bishops and Regulars likewise required that Novice Mistresses be concerned solely with the novices, and hence other offices were not to be given to them.[133] Similarly the *Normae* of 1901, in article 300, forbade to Masters and Mistresses of Novices any office or duty that could impede their care and government of their novices. The Mistress was forbidden to be counselor to the Superioress General. But as often as the council of the Superioress General treated of questions concerning the novices or the novitiate, the Novice Mistress was to be summoned to give her views on the matter in hand.

The present law of the Code repeats the prescription of Clement VIII in almost identical terms.[134] Any specific determination of this general principle by the constitutions of a religious Institute, therefore, are laudable and perfectly legitimate, and hence must be obeyed. Still, the bestowal and acceptance of an office or duty incompatible with that of the Novice Master would not necessarily be invalid, but simply illicit.[135] Yet, if the particular law of an Institute forbade a certain office to be held by the Novice Master under pain of nullity, the bestowal and acceptance of that office would be invalid.

Larraona mentions [136] that if the office to which the Master is elected or nominated is strictly incompatible with his office as Novice Master, then, according to the principle of canon 188, 3°, the office of Novice Master would be tacitly renounced when the Novice Master accepts and takes peaceful possession of the other office. However, this does not seem to be altogether correct. For canon 188, 3°, clearly seems to be treating of cases wherein the two incompatible offices are ecclesiastical offices in the strict sense. It is not clear from the context that offices in the wide sense are included as well.[137]

[133] *AJP,* VI (1863), 2070.

[134] Canon 559, § 3.

[135] Larraona, "Commentarium Codicis"—*CpRM,* XXIII (1942), 261.

[136] *Art. cit., ibid.,* note 1084.

[137] Cf. canon 145, § 2.

Hence, since the office of the Novice Master is an ecclesiastical office only in the wide sense,[138] canon 188, 3°, seems not to apply. Therefore, if a Novice Master were to accept and take peaceful possession of an office incompatible with his office as Novice Master, the acceptance would be illicit, and even invalid if the constitutions so declared it. But he could not be considered as tacitly renouncing his office as Novice Master.

This law freeing the Master and his assistant from incompatible offices is a guarantee against the higher Superiors' act of imposing such tasks upon the Master and his *Socius* as are likely to impede the proper government of the novitiate. Hence, offers of such offices should be refused.[139]

It should be noted that the Code requires the Master and his *Socius* to be free of all offices and duties that *can* impede their care and government of the novices.[140] Hence, if the office can easily become a hindrance to the fulfillment of the Master's obligations to the novices, it should not be imposed on him. If he already has such an office, even though it has not yet actually proved a hindrance, but it prudently can be said that it *could* hinder him, then such an office must be regarded incompatible and ought to be renounced by the Master.[141] It follows from this that the term "offices" as used in canon 559, § 3, must be taken in the wide sense as well as in the strict.[142]

Since, if the Novice Master were the ordinary or habitual confessor for the novices, there would be a danger of his using knowledge acquired through confession in the external government of the novitiate, the Code wisely departs from the legislation of Clement VIII. This latter had required that the Novice Master be the ordi-

[138] Canon 145, § 1.

[139] Meynard, *Réponses canoniques,* p. 207; Larraona, "Commentarium Codicis"—*CpRM,* XXIII (1942), 261.

[140] "Uterque ab omnibus officiis oneribusque vacare debet, quae novitiorum curam et regimen impedire valeant."—Canon 559, § 3.

[141] Cf. Larraona, "Commentarium Codicis"—*CpRM,* XXIII (1942), 261-262.

[142] Cf. canons 145, §§ 1 and 2; Larraona, *art. cit.,* p. 261; Blat, *Ius de Religiosis,* p. 342.

nary confessor of the novices under his care.[143] Accordingly the Code declares the offices of ordinary and habitual confessor incompatible with that of the Novice Master and the *Socius*.[144] The conditions on which the Master or the *Socius* may in an extraordinary case hear the confession of a novice subject to them will be discussed in a later chapter.[145]

The commentators usually consider the general types of duties and offices that appear to be incompatible with the office of the Master and his assistant. The duties from which these officials are often exempt vary in different communities, in dependence largely upon the nature of the community and the kind of work in which it is engaged. The constitutions often dispense them from certain duties, not so much because these could interfere with the care of the novices, but rather because the Master and the *Socius* are considered to be already sufficiently burdened with their respective offices.

It seems altogether equitable that the Master and his assistant be exempt from such duties as taking their turn at waiting at the community table, reading at table, and so on. Care should be taken that they be not sent out of the novitiate frequently on business pertaining to the community at large. Otherwise there is danger that the time which should be devoted to the care of the novices will be too greatly curtailed. Especially should lengthy and frequent absences be guarded against. If either the Master or his assistant be absent habitually at stated times, then the other should always be present in the novitiate.[146] Hence it seems that they should not be engaged outside the monastery by way of regular practice for the hearing of confessions or for the preaching of sermons.

Among the offices which clearly seem incompatible with that of the Novice Master are: the major offices in the religious Institute, such as those of the Superior General, of the Provincial, of the

[143] Clemens VIII, const. *"Cum ad regularem,"* 19 mart. 1603, § 10—*Fontes*, n. 189.

[144] Canon 891.

[145] Chap. V, art. 2.

[146] Berutti, *De Religiosis*, p. 181; Larraona, "Commentarium Codicis"—*CpRM*, XXIII (1942), 262-264.

Abbot of a monastery *sui iuris,* and so on. The office of Counselor to the Superior General and even to the Provincial Superior seems likewise to imply a status of incompatibility. Article 300 of the *Normae* of 1901 explicitly excluded the Novice Master and Mistress from holding the office of General Counselor or Consultor. Many recent congregations have included this prescription in their constitutions.[147]

It appears, however, that the size of the religious Institute could be a factor for the determination whether or not the office of counselor is actually incompatible with that of the Novice Master. In a small province, for instance, the Master might well be one of the Provincial Superior's counselors apart from all likelihood that this office could hinder him in his duties as Master. It should be noted, too, that an office could be compatible with that of the *Socius,* but incompatible with that of the Novice Master.[148]

The question whether or not the Novice Master can at the same time be the local Superior of the novitiate house is of special interest. In the 1912 proposed schema of the Code canon 432 expressly stated that neither the Master nor the *Socius* could be the local Superior if this would impede the care due to the novices.[149] However, the present law has omitted this phrase, evidently because the novitiate house could very well be a distinct and separate house for the novices alone. In such a case there would be no danger that the office of local Superior would interfere with the duties of the Novice Master. Indeed, in those Institutes in which the two offices are joined or contemplated as being joined, this unification of the two offices in the person of the Novice Master is usually limited to the cases wherein the novitiate is a separately constituted house.[150]

Even as regards a religious house where professed members as well as novices are resident, the authors quite generally agree that

[147] Larraona, "Commentarium Codicis"—*CpRM,* XXIII (1942), 262.

[148] Coronata, *Institutiones,* I, n. 585.

[149] Cf. Larraona, "Commentarium Codicis"—*CpRM,* XXIII (1942), 251-252.

[150] Larraona, "Consultatio"—*CpR,* II (1921), 292.

there is no absolute and necessary incompatibility between the two offices. Moreover, the customs and constitutions of many Institutes support this view.[151]

Nervegna, writing before the promulgation of the Code, seems to be about the only author to maintain that the two offices are in practice incompatible.[152] Prümmer (1866-1931) was of the opinion that the two offices should be united only in exceptional cases.[153] Jansen, though admitting that the union of the two offices is not directly forbidden as long as there result no encroachments on the Master's duties toward the novices, holds that it is more in consonance with the spirit of the law that the two offices be separate.[154] Schaefer[155] and Vidal (1867-1938)[156] draw an argument from canon 530, § 1, which forbids religious Superiors to exact a manifestation of conscience from their subjects. They argue that the spiritual formation of the novices can hardly be achieved without the practice of the manifestation of conscience. Hence, for the sake of forestalling the restrictions that would otherwise bind him, the Novice Master ought not be appointed local Superior.[157]

In conclusion, therefore, it seems correct to say that the office of local Superior is not necessarily incompatible with that of the Master of novices. Still, it appears more advisable that the two offices be kept distinct even in cases wherein the novitiate is a separate house independent of a community of professed religious. When the novitiate constitutes a section of a large religious house with other sections, whose members, for example, are engaged in ministerial works, the Novice Master must not be the local Superior.

[151] Cf. Coronata, *Institutiones,* I, n. 585; Raus, *Institutiones Canonicae* (2. ed., Lugduni-Parisiis: Vitte, 1931), p. 304; Pejška, *Ius Canonicum Religiosorum,* p. 95; Wernz-Vidal, *Ius Canonicum,* III, n. 283, note 30; Larraona, "Commentarium Codicis"—*CpRM,* XXIII (1942), 253.

[152] *De Jure Practico Regularium* (Romae, 1900), pp. 104-105.

[153] *Manuale Iuris Canonici,* n. 211.

[154] *Ordensrecht,* pp. 171-172.

[155] *De Religiosis,* p. 531.

[156] *Ius Canonicum,* III, n. 282, note 30.

[157] For a discussion of the application of canon 530, § 1, to the Master of novices, cf. *infra* Chap. V, art. 1, C.

Otherwise, in such cases, the Master could hardly attend to his duties and obligations as Superior without at the same time jeopardizing the proper care and the efficient government of the novices. These cases clearly seem to be included in the phrase of the law "he must be free from all offices which *can* impede the care and the government of the novices." [158]

[158] Canon 559, § 3; cf. Larraona, "Consultatio"—*CpR,* II (1921), 291-299; Voltas, "Consultatio"—*CpR,* II (1921), 220-221.

CHAPTER IV

THE GOVERNMENT OF THE NOVITIATE

Article 1. The Novice Master's Relation to the Superiors

Before the seventeenth century the law had not determined the relation of the Novice Master to his Superiors. In treating of the training of the novices the law had stressed the responsibility of the higher Superiors rather than that of the Novice Master.[1]

With the promulgation of the Constitution *Cum ad regularem* it became clear that the Novice Master had full and absolute power in the government of the novitiate and in the training of the novices. A few obvious exceptions were made. These allowed the major Superiors, Visitors and even the local Superior some authority in this matter. But under no pretext whatsoever aside from these exceptions was anyone else permitted to interfere in the government of the novitiate.[2] However, the Clementine Constitution did not determine to what extent the Superiors could interfere in the government of the novitiate. The present legislation of the Code is more specific and detailed in this matter.[3]

Still, though the Novice Master was assured freedom of action in his government of the novitiate, his office remained a directive one. The law did not constitute him a *praelatus,* nor did it grant him ecclesiastical jurisdiction over the novices.[4]

[1] Provincial Council of Cambrai (1565), tit. XVIII, c. XIV—Mansi, XXX, 1419; Provincial Synod of Manfredonia (1567), tit. *de monasteriis*—Mansi, XXXV B, 891.

[2] Clemens VIII, const. *"Cum ad regularem,"* 19 mart. 1603, § 9: "Habeat etiam Magister plenam, et absolutam potestatem circa Novitiorum institutionem, ac Novitiatus regimen, ita ut nemini (Visitatoribus, ac Superioribus maioribus, vel etiam localibus exceptis) quovis colore se ingerere liceat."—*Fontes,* n. 189; cf. S.C. Ep. et Reg., *Comen.,* 16 mart. 1593, ad 4—*Fontes,* n. 1479.

[3] Canon 561, § 1.

[4] Piatus Montensis, *Praelectiones Juris Regularis,* I, 119.

Canon 561, § 1, of the present law declares that to the Novice Master alone belongs the right and the duty of caring for the formation of the novices, and he alone has full charge of the government of the novitiate. It follows, therefore, that only he is in the fullest sense the spiritual director and instructor of the novices, as well as their immediate and exclusive superior in all things pertaining to the government of the novitiate.[5] Hence, the novices are subject to his power, and accordingly are bound to obey him.[6]

Since this right belongs exclusively to the Novice Master, under no pretext whatsoever can anyone else interfere in the care and government of the novices and the novitiate, except those Superiors and canonical Visitors to whom the constitutions give authority in this matter.[7] Since this is not only a right but also a personal duty of the Master, he cannot allow or depute another to mingle in the affairs of the novitiate. The *Socius* to the Novice Master is an assistant to him, and has only such authority as the Master gives him. He cannot claim or arrogate to himself any other authority than this.[8]

By the care and formation of the novices is meant the instruction in everything pertaining to the religious life as it is led according to the rule of the community concerned. This includes the probation of the novices whereby the genuineness of their vocation is determined, and also their exercise in the Christian virtues, especially those which are required for leading the particular form of religious life to which they aspire.[9]

By the government of the novitiate is meant the regimen of that section of the house which is designated for the novices, and not the novitiate as a religious house. The government of this latter belongs to the local Superior, and in matters pertaining to the whole house or community as such the Novice Master, as well as

[5] Cf. Larraona, "Consultatio"—*CpR,* II (1921), 294-299.

[6] Canon 561, § 2.

[7] Canon 561, § 1.

[8] Cf. canons 561, § 1; 559, § 2; Schaefer, *De Religiosis,* p. 532; Larraona, "Commentarium Codicis"—*CpRM,* XXIV (1943), 31.

[9] Cf. Larraona, "Commentarium Codicis"—*CpRM,* XXIV (1943), 31.

the novices, is subject to the local Superior.[10] The regimen of the novitiate does not include the regimen of the internal sacramental forum, granted simply that the Novice Master is a priest. This is explicitly excluded from the sphere of the Master's domain by canon 891. But the regimen of the internal non-sacramental forum is not excluded.[11]

Though the law reserves the government of the novitiate to the Novice Master, it makes two obvious exceptions. Those canonical Visitors and Superiors to whom the constitutions grant this power may intervene in the government of the novitiate.[12] The canonical Visitors, whether ordinary or delegated, general or provincial, as long as their authority or mandate legitimately extends to the novitiate, undoubtedly can and should investigate everything pertaining to the novitiate and, if need be, make corrections within the limits of their power.[13]

Usually the constitutions indicate which of the major Superiors have a right to intervene in matters concerning the novitiate. This power is concerned with their vigilance over the Novice Master in his duties and obligations toward the novices. This power also includes the right of visitation and correction, and the right to be kept informed on the status of the novitiate and the novices. The Master in turn is bound to obey the precepts and counsel of the Superiors and of legitimate Visitors. This is a necessary requisite to offset any negligence on the part of the Master, and to prevent abuses.

Yet it is possible that such a Superior could violate the law of unity of direction which the Church certainly desires in the novitiate. This could happen if he frequently and unnecessarily would substitute himself in place of the Novice Master on the pretext of doing greater good.[14] Even if the constitutions make no mention of a right of vigilance as belonging to the major Superiors and canon-

[10] Canon 561, § 1.

[11] Larraona, "Commentarium Codicis"—*CpRM,* XXIV (1943), 32.

[12] Canon 561, § 1.

[13] Larraona, "Commentarium Codicis"—*CpRM,* XXIV (1943), 35.

[14] Cf. Vermeersch-Creusen, *Epitome,* I, n. 663; Jansen, *Ordensrecht,* pp. 171-172; Larraona, "Consultatio"—*CpR,* II (1921), 294-299.

ical Visitors, they nevertheless undoubtedly possess this authority. This follows not only from the very nature of the Institute as a society, but likewise from the prescriptions of the common law implicitly expressed by canon 561, § 2.[15]

Concerning the local Superior of the house of novitiate, it must be noted that the common law grants him no authority whatsoever in matters pertaining to the novitiate as such. The constitution of Clement VIII differed in this regard from the present law.[16] But, as Larraona remarks,[17] it gradually became customary in religious institutes to take from the local Superior all authority in these matters and to reserve it to the major Superiors exclusively. Therefore, unless the constitutions of an Institute expressly grant the local Superior authority to intervene in matters concerning the novitiate as such, he has no authority over the Novice Master and the novices in these matters.

Coronata is of the opinion that the local Superior is not absolutely excluded by the common law.[18] He considers the question especially from the viewpoint of custom. If the local Superior has some right of intervention in these matters by custom, he asks, would not the force of this custom be equivalent to that of the constitutions, particularly in cases where no mention of these matters is made in the constitutions themselves. Both Schaefer[19] and Larraona[20] correctly admit that the local Superior could have the right of intervening in matters concerning the novitiate by reason of custom. But since the Code clearly seems to have departed from the old law, such a custom would have to be one legitimately established since the promulgation of the Code, and according to the norms of the law, if it is to have the force of law. Therefore, since the Code has not yet been in force forty years, any customary action on the part of local Superiors in this regard must still be con-

[15] Cf. Larraona, "Commentarium Codicis"—*CpRM,* XXIV (1943), 33-34.

[16] Clemens VIII, const. *"Cum ad regularem,"* 19 mart. 1603, § 9—*Fontes,* n. 189.

[17] *Art. cit.*

[18] *Institutiones,* I, n. 585, 2° and note 6.

[19] *De Religiosis,* p. 532.

[20] "Commentarium Codicis"—*CpRM,* XXIV (1943), 34, and note 117.

sidered an infraction of the law and not yet a legitimately established custom with legal force.[21]

Aside from the case of custom which might in time acquire the force of law, therefore, and aside from the case of an express grant of power by the constitutions, the local Superior has no power whatsoever in matters concerning the novitiate and the Novice Master as such.[22]

According to the norm of canon 561, § 1, however, in matters pertaining to the general discipline of the religious house in which the novitiate is situated, both the Novice Master and the novices, as members of the community, are subject to the local Superior. The commentators usually include under this general discipline such matters as: exercises which are carried on outside the novitiate proper, as processions; exercises performed by the entire community, as community prayers and meditations, the recitation of the Divine Office in common, and the meals taken by the community in the common refectory. These matters of general discipline are quite evident.[23]

Concerning more minute details, such as public penances in the refectory, letter-writing by the novices, their days of recreation and walks permitted to them, the constitutions of each institute must be consulted and observed. For, since the various constitutions differ to some extent in these and similar matters, no hard and fast rule can be formulated. Some constitutions, for example, grant the local Superior no authority to correct the novices even should the fault be public, while others allow the Novice Master to impose penances on the novices only within the novitiate proper.

Creusen says that for penances to be assigned in the refectory, for fixing the days of vacation or the time of a walk, for allowing visits to the parlor, and so on, recourse must be had to the local

[21] Cf. canons 25; 27, § 1.

[22] Cf. Schaefer, *De Religiosis,* p. 532; Beste, *Introductio in Codicem,* p. 375; Vito, *De Religiosis,* p. 205; Vermeersch-Creusen, *Epitome,* I, n. 663; Pejška, *Ius Canonicum Religiosorum,* p. 96; Larraona, "Commentarium Codicis"—*CpRM,* XXIV (1943), 35.

[23] Cf. Prümmer, *Manuale Iuris Canonici,* n. 211; Creusen-Garesché-Ellis, *Religious Men and Women in the Code,* p. 155; Larraona, "Commentarium Codicis"—*CpRM,* XXIV (1943), 35-37.

Superior.[24] This may be true in some communities. But the constitutions of others vary in some or all of these points. Hence the attempt to formulate a general norm in such matters is futile.[25]

Article 2. Nature of the Novice Master's Power

The Constitution *Cum ad regularem* did not state specifically what type of power the Master of Novices enjoyed. It simply stated that he had full and absolute power in the training of the novices and in the government of the novitiate.[26] Speaking of the separation of the lay novices from the choir novices, the Clementine Constitution declared that despite this separation the lay novices were still subject to the Master of Novices and were obliged to obey him.[27]

The Code uses very similar words when it states that to the Novice Master alone belongs the right and the duty of caring for the training of the novices, and to him only does the government of the novitiate belong.[28] It then goes on to state that the novices are subject to the power of the Master and of the Superiors of the Institute, and are bound to obey them.[29]

However, nowhere in the article on the novitiate does the Code express what is the precise nature of the Novice Master's power. Yet one can determine just what is the nature of this power by using the principles of canon 20, especially by investigating the common and constant teaching of authorities.

[24] Creusen-Garesché-Ellis, *Religious Men and Women in the Code*, p. 155.

[25] Some examples of such variations found in various constitutions are given by Larraona—"Commentarium Codicis"—*CpRM*, XXIV (1943), 36-37, notes 1119-1126.

[26] Clemens VIII, const. *"Cum ad regularem,"* 19 mart. 1603, § 9:—"Habeat etiam Magister plenam, et absolutam potestatem circa Novitiorum institutionem, ac Novitiatus regimen . . ."—*Fontes*, n. 189; cf. S.C. Ep. et Reg., *Comen.*, 16 mart. 1593, ad 4—*Fontes*, n. 1479; S.C.C., decr. 21 sept. 1624, § 1—*Fontes*, n. 2454.

[27] Clemens VIII, const. *"Cum ad regularem,"* 19 mart. 1603, § 15: "Illi tamen hac separatione non obstante, Magistro Novitiorum, . . . subditi esse, et obedientiam praestare debeant. . . ."—*Fontes*, n. 189.

[28] Canon 561, § 1: "Uni Magistro ius et officium consulendi novitiorum institutioni, ad ipsumque unum novitiatus regimen spectat. . . ."

[29] Canon 561, § 2.

The first point to be noted is that the Novice Master is not a Superior in the proper canonical sense of the term. This is evident from the fact that canon 561, § 1, clearly distinguishes between the Master and the Superiors, and states that in regard to the general discipline of the house the Novice Master and also the novices are subject to the local Superior. It likewise follows from the fact that the Novice Master as such is not in charge of a religious community. For the Code defines the term religious as those who have pronounced their vows in a religious Institute.[30] Therefore, novices, by the very fact that they are novices, cannot properly be called religious, though they do enjoy the privileges of religious.[31] Hence, it follows that, although the Novice Master is in complete charge of the novitiate and the novices, he is not in charge of a religious community, and accordingly cannot be called a religious Superior in the canonical sense.[32] Nevertheless, being in complete charge of the novices, the Master has authority over them, and the law explicitly states that the novices are subject to his power and are bound to obey him.[33]

Now the formal, proximate object of the virtue of obedience is a precept or command of the Superior; and a Superior is constituted such solely by the power which belongs to him.[34] This is the teaching of Suarez [35] following the doctrine of St. Thomas (1224-1274).[36]

[30] Canon 488, 7°.

[31] Canon 614.

[32] Cf. Creusen-Garesché-Ellis, *Religious Men and Women in the Code,* p. 154.

[33] Canon 561, § 2.

[34] Raus, *De Sacrae Obedientiae Virtute et Voto* (Lugduni: Vitte, 1923), p. 62.

[35] *De Religione,* tract. X, lib. IV, cap. XIV, n. 14: "Obedientiae respicit Superiorem, ut Superior est, non ut est amicus, vel ut prudens ad consulendum, vel sub alia ratione simili; constituitur autem Superior in ratione Superioris per potestatem (dominativam aut jurisdictionis); nam, illa seclusa, homines aequales sunt; ergo obedientia respicit Superiorem, ut utentem sua potestate."

[36] *Sancti Thomae Aquinatis Doctoris Angelici Opera Omnia Iussu Impensaque Leonis XIII, P.M. Edita* (Romae, 1882—); *Summa Theologica* (Romae, 1888-1906), IIa IIae, q. 104, art. 2; *Quodlibetum,* X, a. X: "Obedientia non se extendit ultra potestatem vel jus praelationis, quae quidem secundum regulam limitatur."

It remains therefore to determine what is the precise nature of the power of the Novice Master whereby the novices are bound to obey him.

Canon 501, § 1, in treating of the power of religious Superiors distinguishes between dominative power and the power of jurisdiction. Beside these two powers, many authors speak also of the power which religious Superiors have over their subjects as a result of the vow of obedience made by the subjects. This power is usually referred to as *potestas ex voto*.[37] Finally, some authors speak of a fourth power, which they call domestic or social power.[38]

A. Jurisdiction

The power of ecclesiastical jurisdiction is a public power of the Church as a perfect society whereby it governs its subjects. Canon 196 describes rather than defines jurisdiction.[39] But the explanatory words *seu regiminis* indicate the extensive meaning of the power of jurisdiction as including legislative, judicial and coercive authority. Canonists seek by giving various definitions, to include everything the Code here implies.

Ottaviani defines it as "the public power of governing the baptized in relation to their eternal salvation, bestowed on a legitimate superior by Christ or by the Church through a canonical mission." [40] Since the Church alone has been given this power by Christ, she alone can

[37] *Salmanticenses,* IV, tract. XV, cap. VI, n. 46; Castropalao, *Opus Morale de Virtutibus et Vitiis Contrariis* (7 vols. in 3, Lugduni, 1700), III, tract. XVI, dist. IV, punct. I, n. 4 (hereafter cited as *Opus Morale*); Suarez, *De Religione,* tract. VII, lib. X, cap. VIII, n. 1; Wernz, *Ius Decretalium,* III, n. 652; Raus, *De Sacrae Obedientiae Virtute et Voto,* pp. 62-64; 87-109.

[38] Biederlack-Führich, *De Religiosis,* pp. 52-53; Vermeersch-Creusen, *Epitome,* I, n. 573; Raus, *De Sacrae Obedientiae Virtute et Voto,* pp. 52-53.

[39] "Potestas iurisdictionis seu regiminis quae ex divina institutione est in Ecclesia, alia est fori externi, alia fori interni, seu conscientiae, sive sacramentalis sive extra-sacramentalis."

[40] *Institutiones Iuris Publici Ecclesiastici* (2. ed., 2 vols., Typis Polyglottis Vaticanis: 1935-1936), I, 226: "Potestatem iurisdictionis diximus esse potestatem publicam legitimi superioris a Christo, vel ab Ecclesia per canonicam missionem, concessam, regendi baptizatos in ordine ad salutem aeternam."

bestow it upon others.[41] Her jurisdiction is an authority divinely bestowed primarily upon the Supreme Pontiff, and upon the bishops, and through them upon the other rulers in the Church. Such a participation in her power of jurisdiction has been granted to the religious Superiors of exempt clerical institutions.[42] It has already been seen that the Novice Master is not a religious Superior in the true canonical sense. Therefore, it follows that the power he enjoys cannot be a jurisdictional power.

B. Dominative Power

Jurisdiction is an attribute of a perfect society. In contradistinction to this, the power or authority exercised by the superior of an imperfect society is called dominative power. This power exists in all human societies, and arises either naturally, as does the authority of the head of a family, or as a result of an agreement or contract whereby one person freely subjects himself to the rule of another. By reason of such an agreement the subject binds himself to be directed by his superior in the choice of means conducive to the end of the society.

In all religious communities the Superiors exercise this dominative power over their subjects.[43] But this power does not come from Christ by special grant to the Church as does the jurisdictional power of the Church. It arises radically from the will of those who profess a religious rule and give themselves to a religious Institute with the promise and the obligation of obeying their Superiors according to the rule they have professed.[44]

C. Power Arising from the Vow of Obedience

It seems that religious Superiors have a further power, which arises from the vow of obedience made by their subjects. This is

[41] Canon 196.

[42] Canon 501, § 1.

[43] Canon 501, § 1.

[44] Cf. Suarez, *De Religione*, tract. VII, lib. II, cap. XVIII, n. 5; Vermeersch-Creusen, *Epitome*, I, n. 573; Raus, *De Sacrae Obedientiae Virtute et Voto*, p. 65; Ramos, "De conditione saecularium in domibus religiosorum"—*CpR*, VI (1925), 187-190.

usually referred to as *potestas ex voto.* Many authors maintain that this is a distinct power which religious Superiors enjoy, and which gives them the authority to command their subjects in virtue of the vow of obedience which they have professed. It is distinct from the dominative power, for the promise of obedience made by vow does not give rise to this latter power but rather supposes that it already exists. Hence the vow itself must give the Superior an added authority.[45]

Not all the authors admit this latter point.[46] A detailed discussion need not be given here on this power. For, in any case, the Novice Master cannot possess this power, since the novices are not yet bound by vow.

D. Social or Domestic Power

The Code makes no mention at all of what many authors call social or domestic power. However, this is no reason to pass over a consideration of this type of power. For, according to Biederlack-Führich,[47] this social power has its origin in the natural law itself, and hence the Code supposes its existence. It concerns not religious institutes as such, but rather the virtue of justice and the social or domestic order, so that it is present in every group even of those without vows. Some canonists do not mention this type of power, possibly for the same reason that the Code does not mention it. Other canonists are of the opinion that religious Superiors have this social power as distinct from their dominative power. Still others maintain that it is a power not distinct or separate from dominative power.

Among the older authors, Donatus (+1663)[48] speaks of a "*potestas corporalis, civilis et politica.*" By this he understands that power which pertains to the preservation of domestic order and

[45] Cf. Raus, *De Sacrae Obedientiae Virtute et Voto,* pp. 87-109, for a complete discussion of this matter.

[46] Cf. Marc-Gestermann, *Institutiones Morales Alphonsianae* (17. ed., 2 vols., Lugduni: Vitte, 1922-1923), II, n. 2165 b; n. 2167, note 1.

[47] *De Religiosis,* pp. 54-55.

[48] *Rerum Regularium Praxis Resolutoria* (4 vols. in 2, Coloniae Agrippinae, 1728), tom. II, pars II, tract. VI, q. 13, n. 11.

serves for the stabilization of a legitimate group formed of a number of men for a specific end or purpose. This is necessary, for in any legitimate group someone must be at its head to govern the other members, and it is necessary that there exist someone to whom they must in some way be subject for the sake of good order and for the preservation of the entire group.

Lessius (1554-1623) likewise speaks of a *potestas politica.*[49] His manifold distinctions, however, are somewhat confusing. Yet, by this "political power" he seems to mean the jurisdictional power of the civil authority in contradistinction to the jurisdiction of the Church. Grandclaude (1826-1900) also speaks of a domestic or civil power.[50] However, he identifies this power with dominative power. Finally, Lehmkuhl (1834-1918), in classifying the various types of power belonging to a religious Superior, mentions domestic power as a power distinct both from dominative power and from the power of jurisdiction.[51] He expressly says that it is to this power of the Superior that novices are subject, while the professed religious are subject to the dominative power of the Superiors, and, in the case of clerical exempt institutes, to his jurisdiction.[52]

Among the authors who have treated this subject since the promulgation of the Code, Brandys likewise gives this threefold division.[53] By reason of the domestic power, he says, the Superior has a special right as head of the religious community over all those who belong to that group, whether they belong permanently or temporarily. This domestic power, according to Brandys, is not very dissimilar to that exercised by a father of a family. But he adds

[49] *De Iustitia et Iure Caeterisque Virtutibus Cardinalibus* (4 vols. in 1, Lugduni, 1653), lib. II, c. XLI, dubit. I, n. 10, 80; c. XLVI, dubit. IV, n. 24 sq.

[50] *Jus Canonicum* (3 vols., Parisiis, 1882), II, 421-422.

[51] *Theologia Moralis* (10. ed., 2 vols., Friburgi Brisgoviae, 1902), I, 325-326.

[52] "Prima praelati potestas est *domestica,* cui etiam subjacent novitii et famuli, at relate ad religiosum haec quodammodo absorbetur a secunda *dominativa* potestate, qua Superior nomine Dei et religiosi ordinis jubet; tertia est potestas *jurisdictionis,* qua Superior ut praelatus *ecclesiasticus* potitur, quum quasi-episcopalem potestatem exerceat."

[53] *Kirchliches Rechtsbuch* (2. ed., Paderborn: 1920), pp. 196-197.

that this power is not dominative power. His reason for this is that this latter power belongs to the religious Superior only by reason of the religious profession of his subjects.[54]

Führich also gives this threefold division, but calls the last power social or economic.[55]

Vermeersch-Creusen likewise speak of the domestic power necessary for the preservation of the domestic order.[56] Schaefer cites several authors who say the religious Superior has this domestic or social power, and apparently agrees with the opinion. He adds that in a religious Institute this power arises from the voluntary entrance into the religious Institute.[57]

It seems preferable to call this power social rather than domestic power, since it has its origin in the very nature of society.[58] Every society must have someone to govern it, who thus exercises authority over the members at least in regard to matters pertaining to the achieving of the end for which the society or group has been formed. By his authority a superior may govern his subjects directly and thus rule over the will of the subjects, or through it he may exercise a more or less extrinsic control over the activity of the subjects. Thus by natural law children are subject entirely to the authority of their parents, for the reason that they were born into the society which is the family. Likewise, professed religious are subject to the authority of their legitimate Superiors, for the reason that they have freely submitted their will to the latter by their act of profession. This authority of the Superiors is exercised through their dominative power.

So, too, those who freely enter into a social group must submit themselves to a degree to the authority which directs the group. The superiors then have the right to demand of the subjects what-

[54] *Ibid.*, p. 31.

[55] "Das Ordensrecht nach dem *Codex Iuris Canonici*"—*TPQ*, LXXII (1919), 178; cf. Biederlack-Führich, *De Religiosis*, pp. 54-55.

[56] *Epitome*, I, nn. 573, 666.

[57] *De Religiosis*, pp. 221-222.

[58] Raus, *De Sacrae Obedientiae Virtute et Voto*, p. 115; cf. Biederlack-Führich, *De Religiosis*, pp. 52, 203; Führich, "Das Ordensrecht nach dem *Codex Iuris Canonici*"—*TPQ*, LXXII (1919), 178.

ever is required for the maintenance of the group or the society. However, such an authority does not extend directly to the will of the subordinates, but only to those actions of the subjects which are necessary for the attainment of the purpose of the society. Such, for example, is the dependence of workmen on their employer, of novices and postulants on their Superiors. Though the Code does not assign any definite name to this type of private authority, the greater number of canonists calls it a social or a domestic power.[59]

Social power, then, may be defined as "that which naturally belongs to a superior as the head of a legitimate society, even a lesser society, and which he necessarily has for the purpose of preserving the domestic order within the limits of the society's purpose." [60]

Canonists point out that by reason of his social power a Superior can command only those things that are necessary for the preservation of the domestic order. In respect to religious Superiors, therefore, it might be looked upon as an imperfect and very limited dominative power. Indeed, it is absorbed, as Lehmkuhl expresses it,[61] by the dominative power of the religious Superior when his subjects are professed members of the institute. It follows from this that the clearest and most noteworthy example of social power is found in the power which the Novice Master and religious Superiors exercise over novices and postulants.[62]

This can be seen from the fact that many of the commentators on the Decretal Law maintained that novices were bound by the statutes and precepts of the rule of the religious Institute to which they aspired. Likewise they were subject to the authority and the commands of their Superiors.[63] These commentators quite generally

[59] Cf. Raus, *De Sacrae Obedientiae Virtute et Voto,* p. 115; Creusen-Garesché-Ellis, *Religious Men and Women in the Code,* p. 34.

[60] Potestas socialis "est facultas quae Superiori naturaliter competit tanquam capiti alicujus legitimi coetus, quamque ipse necessario habet ad ordinem domesticum servandum etiam in minore societate intra limites finis intenti."—Raus, *op. cit.,* p. 116.

[61] *Theologia Moralis,* pp. 325-326; cf. Schaefer, *De Religiosis,* p. 231.

[62] In clerical exempt religious Institutes, however, the Superiors also have the power of ecclesiastical jurisdiction over the novices and postulants. Cf. canon 875, § 1; 1245, § 3.

[63] Cf. Donatus, *Rerum Regularium Praxis Resolutoria,* tom. II, pars II,

defend their position by arguing that novices are not bound *per se* and in conscience to obey the rule, since they are not religious in the proper meaning of the word, having not yet made their profession of vows. Only professed members are bound to obey the rule *ex iustitia.* Indeed the Decretal Law itself expressly stated that novices were not really religious, since they were only aspiring to the religious state.[64]

Still, even though not bound to observe the rule in strict subjection and as a matter of conscience, novices are bound, as some of the commentators expressed it, *ex quadam decentia et urbanitate,* that is, out of decency and courtesy. The reason assigned for this was that, since the novitiate is a place of probation and trial, unless the novices observe the rule and obey the Superiors they can hardly test that particular form of the religious life properly and sufficiently. Nor can the Institute sufficiently prove the novices. Moreover, the good order of the community demands that they obey.

Most of these commentators also quote the aphorism from the Decretal Law to the effect that whoever takes up a life similar to that led by others should follow a similar discipline.[65]

According to these commentators this was the common opinion among the authors. Certainly it was the express legislation of the Church, as contained in the Clementine Constitution of 1603.[66] Similarly canon 561, § 2, of the present law states that the novices

tract. VI, q. 11-13; Schmalzgrueber, *Jus Ecclesiasticum Universum,* lib. III, tit. XXXI, nn. 85-87; Reiffenstuel, *Jus Canonicum Universum,* lib. III, tit. XXXI, nn. 124-126; Castropalao, *Opus Morale,* pars III, tract. XVI, disput. I, punct. X, nn. 5-9; *Salmanticenses,* tom. IV, tract. XV, cap. III, n. 79; Pirhing, *Compendium Juris Canonici* (Dilingae, 1690), lib. III, tit. XXXI, sect. II, § 6; Suarez, *De Religione,* tract. VII, lib. V, c. XVI, nn. 1, 2, 18; Wernz, *Ius Decretalium,* III, n. 637.

[64] C. 21, *de sententia excommunicationis, suspensionis et interdicti,* V, 11, in VI°.

[65] "Si qui similem cum aliis vitam suscipiunt, similem sentiant in legibus disciplinam."—c. 3, X, *de statu monachorum et canonicorum regularium,* III, 35. In the Decretals this canon is attributed to Alexander III (1159-1181), but the notes of the Friedberg edition indicate that it was issued by Clement III (1187-1191). Cf. Jaffé, *Regesta,* n. 13847 (8914).

[66] Clemens VIII, const. *"Cum ad regularem,"* 19 mart. 1603, §§ 9, 15—*Fontes,* n. 189.

are subject to the power of the Novice Master and of the Superiors of the religious Institute, and are bound to obey them. Most of the present day commentators explain this obligation in substantially the same way as did the older commentators.[67]

Now, since the novices are bound to obey the Novice Master and the Superiors, these officials must in turn have a power correlative to the obligation of their subjects. Since the Superiors exercise the dominative power over their professed subjects, and since this power arises only by reason of the act of religious profession,[68] the only alternative is that the power of the Master and of the Superiors over the novices is this social power.

Some canonists in treating the power of the Novice Master content themselves with merely repeating the ruling of canon 561, § 2, and state that the novices are subject to the power of the Master and are bound to obey him. But they do not inquire into the precise nature of this power. A few canonists are of the opinion that the power of the Novice Master, as well as that of the Superiors over the novices, is the dominative power.[69] Finally, a number of canonists maintains that the power of the Novice Master is not the dominative, but rather the domestic or social power.[70]

In summarizing this article on the power of the Novice Master, one may state that, although the novices are not directly bound to obey the Rule and the Superiors in conscience in the same way as are

[67] Cf. Wernz-Vidal, *Ius Canonicum,* III, n. 289; Vermeersch-Creusen, *Epitome,* I, n. 666; Schaefer, *De Religiosis,* pp. 544-545. However, Schaefer here says that the novices are bound not merely out of honesty and courtesy, but also because of a tacit pact or agreement.

[68] Cf. canon 501, § 1.

[69] Molitor, *Religiosi Iuris Capita Selecta* (Ratisbonae, 1909), pp. 247-248; Blat, *Ius de Religiosis,* p. 344; cf. Pejška, *Ius Canonicum Religiosorum,* p. 97; Prümmer, *Manuale Iuris Canonici,* p. 249; Cappello, *Summa Iuris Canonici* (3 vols., Romae: Apud Aedes Universitatis Gregorianae, 1928-1936), I, n. 608, 2.

[70] Schaefer, *De Religiosos,* p. 533; Vermeersch-Creusen, *Epitome,* I, n. 411; Raus, *De Sacrae Obedientiae Virtute et Voto,* p. 109 sq.; Biederlack-Führich, *De Religiosis,* pp. 54-55; Beste, *Introductio in Codicem,* pp. 375-376; Brandys, *Kirchliches Rechtsbuch,* pp. 31, 197; Creusen-Garesché-Ellis, *Religious Men and Women in the Code,* p. 34; Coronata, *Institutiones,* I, n. 602, II, 1°, note 5.

the professed religious, they are still bound to obey the Master and the Superiors by reason of the social power exercised by these officials, and by reason of the express statement of canon 561, § 2.

The Novice Master cannot impose ecclesiastical penalties upon the novices for transgressions committed by them, for the power of jurisdiction is required for the infliction of such penalties.[71] However, he can impose disciplinary penances upon them. Furthermore, the novices are subject to the penances established by the rule for the transgression of its precepts, and, in clerical exempt religious Institutes, to the ecclesiastical penalties established by the rule or threatened by the Superiors.[72]

Since the Novice Master's power is not dominative, he cannot nullify the non-reserved private vows which a novice may have made previous to his entrance into the novitiate. In a clerical exempt religious Institute, however, the Superiors could dispense the novice from such a vow.[73] The Novice Master, however, could suspend the obligation of such a vow provided that the fulfillment of the vow would be prejudicial to the order of the novitiate.[74]

A final question concerning the obedience due the Novice Master is proposed by the prescription of canon 633, § 1. This canon states that a professed religious who transfers to another religious Institute must first make the year of novitiate in the new Institute before making his act of religious profession. During the novitiate, the law states, such a novice is bound to obey the Superiors and the Novice Master even by reason of the vow of obedience made in the first religious Institute.

According to Goyeneche, who alone of the authors consulted treats the question at any length,[75] the Superiors of the new Institute cannot command the novice by reason of his vow to do anything which exceeds the limits of the vow. However, they can command

[71] Cf. canons 2220, § 1; 501, § 1.

[72] Prümmer, *Manuale Iuris Canonici*, pp. 282-283.

[73] Canons 1312, § 1; 1313, 2°; cf. canon 1320 on promissory oaths.

[74] Canon 1312, § 2; cf. Berutti, *De Religiosis*, p. 51. These same principles obtain in reference to non-reserved private vows made during the novitiate.—Cf. Schaefer, *De Religiosis*, p. 239.

[75] "De Transitu ad aliam Religionem"—*CpR*, II (1921), 116-124.

anything within the limits of the Rule and constitutions of the new Institute, not by reason of the vow, but rather because of the power and authority they exercise over the novices.[76]

Concerning formal precepts of obedience, it seems that the Superiors can impose these only if they are within the limits of the constitutions of the religious Institute in which the religious is now a novice. This is true even though the precept, exceeding the limits of these constitutions, is still within the ambit of the vow as made in the former Institute. The reason for this is not that the ambit of the vow is exceeded, but that the Superiors lack the power to give such a command. This power does not and cannot go beyond the province of the Rule and constitutions. Hence the Superiors have no power to give a formal precept of obedience concerning a matter that is beyond the limits of the Rule and constitutions of their own Institute, even though it may still be within the limits of the vow itself.[77]

The Superiors of the new Institute, therefore, in relation to the novice here considered, can by reason of his vow command only those things which are within the ambit of the vow and, moreover, are also contained within the Rule or constitutions of the new Institute. These same principles, it seems, apply also to the Novice Master, since canon 633, § 1, states that such a novice is bound to obey the Master even in virtue of his vow of obedience.

Article 3. The Administrative Relation of the Novice Master to the Novices

A. Admission and Dismissal of Novices

The duty of admitting novices to the novitiate never belonged to the Novice Master. On the contrary, it was always a recognized duty of the Superiors.[78] Nor could the Novice Master dismiss a novice,

[76] Goyeneche, *art. cit.*, pp. 117-118.

[77] Goyeneche, *art. cit.*, p. 118.

[78] Cf. Sixtus V, const. *"Cum de omnibus,"* 26 nov. 1587 § 2—*Fontes*, n. 162; *idem*, const. *"Ad Romanum,"* 21 oct. 1588, § 7—*Fontes*, n. 164; Gregorius XIV, const. *"Circumspecta,"* 15 mart. 1591, § 3—*Fontes*, n. 170; Clemens VIII, const. *"Cum ad regularem,"* 19 mart. 1603, § 5—*Fontes*, n. 189; S.C.

since that too was regarded as an exercise of power reserved to the higher Superiors.[79] However, before a novice was admitted to profession the Novice Master was obliged to report on the novice's conduct and vocation, and to declare whether he believed before God that the novice could safely be admitted to profession.[80] The law regarded this matter of such importance that severe penalties were inflicted by it on those who violated its prescriptions. However, the profession of a novice admitted to vows without the formalities of the decree *Regulari disciplinae* being duly observed was merely an illicit, not an invalid, profession.[81]

It can be seen therefore that, despite his lack of power to dismiss a novice, the Master did play an important rôle in the admission of novices to religious profession or in their rejection from it. This grave responsibility was extended shortly before the promulgation of the Code. The Sacred Congregation of Religious issued a decree forbidding admission to the novitiate and to profession of those who had been expelled from even lay colleges because of lack of proper character or for certain other offenses; of those who had been dismissed for any reason whatsoever from seminaries or colleges, whether ecclesiastical or religious; of those who, as professed members or as novices, had been dismissed from another Order or Congregation, or who had obtained a dispensation from their vows; and finally of those who, as professed members or as novices, had been dismissed and wished to be received again into the same or another province of their former Order or Congregation.[82] In the following year these norms were likewise issued for Institutes of women religious.[83] However, it seems that these regulations did not apply

super Statu Regularium, decr. "*Regulari disciplinae,*" 25 ian. 1848, pars I, ad III-V—*Fontes,* n. 4376; Aichner, *Compendium Juris Ecclesiastici* (6. ed., Brixinae, 1887), pp. 464-465.

[79] Cf. S.C. super Statu Regularium, decr. "*Regulari disciplinae,*" 25 ian. 1848, pars II, ad III-V—*Fontes,* n. 4376; S.C. Ep. et Reg., declar. 25 nov. 1904—*Il Monitore Ecclesiastico* (Romae, 1876—), XVII (1905), 62.

[80] S.C. super Statu Regularium, decr. "*Regulari disciplinae,*" 25 ian. 1848, pars II, ad IV—*Fontes,* n. 4376.

[81] Bizzarri, *Collectanea,* p. 843.

[82] S.C. de Religiosis, decr. 7 sept. 1909—*Fontes,* n. 4396.

[83] S.C. de Religiosis, declar. 4 ian. 1910—*Fontes,* n. 4399.

to diocesan religious Institutes, though they were evidently excellent directive norms for such congregations.[84]

These laws were binding primarily on the Superiors whose right and duty it was to admit or reject candidates to the novitiate or to profession. Yet they did impose a grave responsibility upon the Novice Master, inasmuch as he played an important part in the actual rejection of the candidates. Any law requiring testimonials concerning former novices was of intimate concern to the Novice Master.[85]

The question arose whether or not a Master of Novices acted lawfully if he advised a novice to leave the novitiate when the novice really merited dismissal. This was evidently an evasion which frustrated the very purpose of the law, namely, to prevent any religious Institute from accepting such candidates as had merited dismissal from another Institute. Though admitting that the practice was an evasion of the law, Vermeersch (1858-1936) hesitated to condemn a Novice Master who so advised a novice to leave the novitiate.[86] However, the Holy See soon afterwards manifested its opposition to such a practice by declaring that those who had not been *formally* dismissed, but only *equivalently,* were unlawfully though validly admitted to another novitiate.[87]

The Master of Novices was further forbidden by the decree *Regulari disciplinae* to act as examiner in admitting his own novices to profession. However, this seems to have been a safeguard for conscience rather than a curtailment of the Master's activities.[88]

[84] Cf. Freriks, *Religious Congregations in their External Relations,* The Catholic University of America Canon Law Studies, n. 1 (Washington, D. C.: The Catholic University of America, 1916), p. 52.

[85] Cf. S.C. de Religiosis, declar. 5 apr. 1910, ad II—*Fontes,* n. 4400.

[86] *Periodica de Re Canonica et Morali utili praesertim Religiosis et Missionariis* (Brugis, 1905—), V, (1913), 56. (Hereafter this periodical will be cited as *Periodica.*)

[87] S.C. de Religiosis, declar. 5 apr. 1910, ad III—*Fontes,* n. 4400. The prescriptions of this section of the declaration have been incorporated into the present law in canons 544, § 3, and 545, §§ 1 and 4. Admitting a candidate without the testimonials required by these canons would certainly be an infraction of the law.

[88] S.C. Ep. et Reg., 14 iun. 1904—*Il Monitore Ecclesiastico,* XVI (1904), 253-254.

The present law likewise reserves to the major Superiors the right to admit the novices both to the novitiate and to profession. The vote of the Superior's council or chapter is required as well, but whether this needs to be a deliberative or merely a consultative vote depends upon the constitutions of each Institute.[89] Similarly, canon 571, § 1, limits the right of dismissing a novice, if this is deemed necessary, to the Superiors or to the Chapter, according to the constitutions. Any just cause warrants such a dismissal. It follows therefore that the Novice Master has no authority to admit candidates to the novitiate or novices to profession, or to dismiss the latter from the novitiate.

Nevertheless the Master is required by the prescription of canon 563 to make a report on each of the novices to the Chapter or the Major Superior, according as the constitutions determine it. This report evidently will have a bearing on the admission of the novices to profession, or on their dismissal from the novitiate. But aside from this the Master has no vote or authority in the matter of admission and dismissal from the novitiate, or of admission to profession.

B. Report on the Novices

The report on the novices which the Novice Master was required by law to make to the higher Superiors naturally was influential in determining the acceptance or the rejection of the novices. According to Martène (1654-1739) such a report was required in the earlier monastic discipline.[90] However, no such report was required by the law of Clement VIII. It was not until 1848 that the law demanded such a report of the Novice Master.[91] The decree issued in that year obliged the Novice Master to give the Provincial a general estimate of the novices' conduct during the novitiate, and a report on

[89] Canon 543.

[90] "Abbas . . . adhuc a dicto magistro debet inquirere de statu et conversatione illorum. . . . Et antequam veniat dies professionis eorum, adhuc abbas debet se informare de magistro illorum."—*De Antiquis Ecclesiae Ritibus*, III, lib. II, cap. II, Ordo VII.

[91] S.C. super Statu Regularium, decr. "*Regulari disciplinae*," 25 ian. 1848, pars II, ad IV—*Fontes*, n. 4376.

their vocation and on their freedom and fitness for entering the religious state, and to declare whether or not he believed before God that the novices could safely be admitted to profession. If the Novice Master could not present this report personally to the Provincial, he was obliged to do it in writing, signing it with his own hand and confirming it by oath.

Later, in 1910, when the Holy See prescribed a certain amount of study in the novitiate, the report to the Superiors had to contain an account of the diligence and progress shown by each novice in the prescribed studies.[92] According to Vermeersch this report on the studies of the novices was seriously to be considered before the admission of the novices to profession. For piety itself might rightly be suspected if the studies were neglected, or at least there might be an indication that the mind lacked a firm determination and that the novice was consequently little fitted for the works of the Institute.[93]

Canon 563 of the present law likewise prescribes that during the year of the novitiate, according to the norms of the constitutions, the Novice Master must render a report on each of the novices to the major Superior or to the Chapter. The prescriptions of this law are more generic than were those of the decree *Regulari disciplinae,* thereby leaving the details of the report to be determined by the constitutions of each Institute. It is in this sense that the phrase "according to the norms of the constitutions," as employed in canon 563, is to be understood. This phrase does not mean that the obligation of making the report is not imposed by the general law, but rather that the manner, time and frequency of making it, what information the report is to contain, and to whom it is to be made, are all determined by the constitutions.[94]

If the constitutions make no specifications regarding the report, then the Master is obliged to make it once during the year of the novitiate. It is to be made to the major Superior or the Chapter

[92] S.C. de Religiosis, decr. 27 aug. 1910, n. 4—*Fontes,* n. 4405.

[93] "De aliqua in noviciatu studiis opera danda"—*Periodica,* V (1913), 197, n. 6.

[94] Schaefer, *De Religiosis,* p. 533; Vermeersch-Creusen, *Epitome,* I, n. 663; Fanfani, *De Iure Religiosorum,* n. 210.

which has the right, according to the constitutions, of dismissing the novices and of admitting them to profession. In such a case, according to Berutti, an oral report made to the competent Superior prior to his final decision whether or not each novice is to be admitted to profession, seems to be sufficient to satisfy the requirements of the common law.[95] But, as will be seen shortly, the better interpretation seems to be that the report must be in writing. Usually, however, the constitutions make specific requisites concerning this report. It is entirely consonant with the law that they require it to be made periodically during the year of novitiate.[96]

The obligation to make this report is a personal one incumbent on the Novice Master. Should the constitutions require an additional report from the *Socius*, or from the local Superior for example, these cannot supply for the one required of the Novice Master by the common law.[97]

The law requires that a separate report on each of the novices be made. A general report on the novices taken collectively does not suffice. There is nothing in the law, however, to forbid the Master to render the individual reports on each novice simultaneously to the competent Superior.[98] Furthermore, not only must the information contained in the reports be kept confidential by both the Master and the Superiors to wnom the report is made,[99] but likewise the Master must take care not to include any matters which he has come to know solely through confidential talks with the novice, or through a manifestation of conscience freely made to him by a novice. In other words, the report is to contain mention of only such matters as pertain to the external forum. It must carefully avoid mentioning anything directly pertaining to the internal forum, the sphere of conscience.[100]

The decree *Regulari disciplinae* required that the report on the

[95] *De Religiosis*, p. 182.

[96] Coronata, *Institutiones*, I, n. 585.

[97] Larraona, "Commentarium Codicis"—*CpRM*, XXIV (1943), 121.

[98] Cf. Larraona, "Commentarium Codicis"—*CpRM*, XXIV (1943), 122.

[99] Vito, *De Religiosis*, p. 207.

[100] Vito, *De Religiosis*, p. 207; Larraona, "Commentarium Codicis"—*CpRM*, XXIV (1943), 121; Goyeneche, "Consultatio"—*CpRM*, XVIII (1937), 95.

novices be made to the Provincial in writing toward the end of every three months.[101] Canon 563 of the Code does not use the words *in scripto,* or *in scriptis* (in writing). Still the words that are used: let him show the report to the Superior (*relationem . . . Superiori . . . exhibeat*), seem to indicate that the report must be in writing. Larraona maintains that this is the better interpretation, but in any case, he says, the report is often required by the various constitutions to be in writing.[102]

Usually, too, the report is to be made four times a year, although some constitutions require it more frequently. The Code makes no special mention regarding the final report to be made by the Novice Master as to the novice's fitness for admission to profession. The decree *Regulari disciplinae,* on the other hand, had ordered that the last report was to be made two months before profession, and the Master was to confirm by oath the truth of what he reported.[103] Particular law frequently makes similar specifications, but they are not demanded by the common law.[104]

The common law supposes only one year of novitiate. It leaves it to the constitutions of the individual Institutes to determine whether or not there shall be a second year.[105] Hence, in treating of the report to be made by the Novice Master, canon 563 is concerned only with the canonical year of the novitiate. To say that this report must also be made during the second year, if such is required, would appear to be imposing an obligation not imposed by the law itself. However, the constitutions of many Institutes which require a second year of novitiate oblige the Master to make his report during both years, as long as the novices are under his care.[106] But unless such an obligation is imposed by particular law, it does not seem to be obligatory by force of the general law.

[101] S.C. super Statu Regularium, decr. "*Regulari disciplinae,*" 25 ian. 1848, pars II, n. II—*Fontes,* n. 4376.

[102] Larraona, "Commentarium Codicis"—*CpRM,* XXIV (1943), 124; 122.

[103] S.C. super Statu Regularium, decr. "*Regulari disciplinae,*" 25 ian. 1848, pars II, n. III—*Fontes,* n. 4376.

[104] Larraona, *art. cit.,* p. 122.

[105] Canon 555, §§ 1, 2.

[106] Larraona, "Commentarium Codicis"—*CpRM,* XXIV (1943), 121.

C. Separation of the Novices

1. Historical Notes

Though it had long been a monastic custom to assign the novices a distinct place in the monastery.[107] the rule of separation was first incorporated into the law by means of the Constitution *Cum ad regularem.* This Constitution ordered that the novitiate was to have its own proper cloister, separate and distinct from that of the professed members of the monastery. Each novice was to have his own cell, or at least there was to be a common dormitory with sufficient beds to accommodate each individual novice. The Master and his *Socius* were to have their cells within the novitiate cloister, or were at least to have a determined place in the dormitory.

Moreover, within the cloister of the novitiate there was to be a designated place where the spiritual conferences were given and where the Master was to instruct the novices. The papal constitution even demanded that this room or hall was to be heated in winter. The novices were also to have their own oratory, if this was possible. Similarly, they were to have their own separate garden, closed off from intruders, where they could recreate. If this was not possible, the novices were permitted to spend their recreation period in the monastery garden used by the professed members.

The Master was charged with the obligation of seeing to it that no externs, even religious of other Orders or even of the same Order, entered the cloister of the novitiate. If need be, the Master could call on the authority of the local Superior to enforce this regulation. At no time and under no pretext was anyone, except the Master, his *Socius* and, if necessary, the Superior of the monastery, to enter the novitiate cloister. If the Superior did enter he was obliged always to have an older religious accompany him. The Master was to keep the key to the novitiate always in his own possession, and he alone for a grave reason could permit entrance to someone otherwise prohibited. The novices were permitted to speak with externs only with the permission of the Master and in his presence.[108]

[107] Cf. *Regula Sancti Benedicti,* cap. 58, 73.

[108] Clemens VIII, const. "*Cum ad regularem,*" 19 mart. 1603, § 8—*Fontes,* n. 189.

The Clementine Constitution further forbade the novices to associate with the professed members of the monastery except in choir, in the church at the time of the divine offices, in processions, and finally in the common refectory at mealtime. They were likewise forbidden to accompany the professed members when the latter journeyed outside the monastery.[109]

Later on the Sacred Congregation of Bishops and Regulars applied these same norms to nuns.[110] Still later, when the same Congregation issued the *Normae* of 1901, it employed the words of the Clementine Constitution almost verbatim in forbidding the novices to associate with the professed religious.[111]

2. Separation of the Choir Novices

The present law, though requiring the separation of the novices from the professed, is not as strict as was the Constitution *Cum ad regularem*. Canon 564, § 1, states that the novitiate, insofar as is possible, be separated from that part of the religious house in which the professed members live. The purpose of this separation is to offset the possibility of interference with the direction of the novices, and, in general, that the end of the novitiate may be properly achieved.[112]

Although the law explicitly mentions only the professed religious, still its meaning seems to be that externs are excluded as well from communing with the novices.[113] It may be questioned, however, whether postulants are also excluded. A response of the Sacred Congregation of Bishops and Regulars cited by Battandier (1850-1921) forbade postulants to live in the novitiate with the novices.[114] The

109 Clemens VIII, const. *"Cum ad regularem,"* 19 mart. 1603, § 13—*Fontes*, n. 189.

110 S.C. Ep. et Reg., *Florentina*, 30 maii 1626—*Fontes*, n. 1724.

111 *Normae*, art. 85. Goyeneche remarks that it is the practice and the wish of the Sacred Congregation of Religious that this article of the *Normae* be expressed in the text of new sets of constitutions submitted to the Sacred Congregation for approval. "Consultatio"—*CpR*, XII (1931), 254, note 4.

112 Cf. canons 561, § 1; 565; Wernz-Vidal, *Ius Canonicum*, III, n. 286.

113 Larraona, "Commentarium Codicis"—*CpRM*, XXIV (1943), 203.

114 S.C. Ep. et Reg., 1 ian. 1862, ad 6um—Battandier, *Guide canonique*, p. 97.

Normae, on the contrary, permitted the postulants to live in the novitiate, but in a place apart from the novices, if this could be done.[115] This ruling, however, was not contained in the decree of the Sacred Congregation of Religious which first established the postulancy as an institute of common law.[116] Nor was it contained in a subsequent decree on the postulancy issued by the Sacred Congregation in the following year.[117] The Code in canon 540, § 1, permits the postulants to live in the novitiate, but there is no express prohibition forbidding them to commune with the novices.

Although the commentators admit this, they nevertheless maintain that it is more in conformity with the spirit of the law that the novices be separated from the postulants. Or at least, these canonists say, the lay postulants, who may live with the lay novices, should be separated from the choir novices and postulants.[118] Goyeneche points out [119] that it is the practice of the commission for the approbation and revision of constitutions to support this view. Yet in some religious Institutes the postulants about to enter the novitiate usually live not only in the novitiate house, but also in the novitiate itself with the novices.[120]

The proper conclusion to this discussion, so it seems, is that, although communication and association between the novices and the postulants does not appear to be forbidden by the Code, still, if the constitutions or customary practice of an Institute require that the groups be separated, then this requisite must be followed as particular law.

In demanding the separation of the novices canon 564, § 1, states this is to be done in as far as it is possible. Thus it tempers the rigor of the Clementine Constitution. Still, when the material segre-

[115] *Normae,* art. 64.

[116] S.C. de Religiosis, decr. 1 ian. 1911—*AAS,* III (1911), 29-36.

[117] S.C. de Religiosis, decr. 15 aug. 1912, nn. 2, 3—*AAS,* IV (1912), 565-566.

[118] Canon 564, § 2; Schaefer, *De Religiosis,* p. 459; Goyeneche, "Consultatio"—*CpR,* XIV (1933), 356; Larraona, "Commentarium Codicis"—*CpRM,* XVI (1935), 308-309.

[119] *Art. cit., loc. cit.*

[120] Larraona, "Commentarium Codicis"—*CpRM,* XXIV (1943), 203, note 1158.

gation of the novices from the other members living in the house is not absolute and complete, there ought to be greater vigilance on the part of the Novice Master to guard against communication or association between the novices and the professed religious.[121] For such association is prohibited as a general rule by the law. Only for a special reason and with the permission of the Novice Master or of the local Superior can there be any association between the novices and the professed.[122] The judgment of what legitimately constitutes a special reason will depend upon the prudence of the Master or the Superior. Close relationship or perhaps even close friendship between a novice and one of the professed members of the Institute seems to be a sufficient reason. A special reason is all that is required by law. A grave cause, as once demanded by the Clementine Constitution,[123] is no longer required.

The obligation of keeping the novices apart from the professed religious is binding even if there are but few novices. But since the law demands it only insofar as it is possible, some authors maintain that it is permissible to allow the novices and the professed to associate at recreation time on certain days, for example, on the more solemn feasts.[124] This would obtain particularly in religious Institutes which are still small and in which communication between the two groups therefore is likely to be more frequent. Indeed, in such a case too severe an isolation of the novices might have serious disadvantages in their character formation.[125] But even in this case the permission of the Master or of the local Superior is required. The permission of either seems sufficient from the wording of the law.[126] Yet, since both the novices and the professed are concerned, it seems more in consonance with the spirit of the law that the per-

[121] Larraona, "Commentarium Codicis"—*CpRM,* XXIV (1943), 204.

[122] Canon 564, § 1.

[123] Clemens VIII, const. *"Cum ad regularem,"* 19 mart. 1603, § 8—*Fontes,* n. 189.

[124] Vermeersch-Creusen, *Epitome,* I, n. 664; Creusen-Garesché-Ellis, *Religious Men and Women in the Code,* p. 156.

[125] Creusen-Garesché-Ellis, *loc. cit.*; Claeys Bouuaert-Simenon, *Manuale Juris Canonici* (3 vols., Vols. I et III, 3. ed., Gandae et Leodii: De Meester, 1930-1931), I, 377; Berutti, *De Religiosis,* p. 169.

[126] Canon 564, § 1.

mission of both be obtained. This is the opinion of Larraona, and he wisely adds that the Master and the Superior ought to discuss the matter between them before granting permission.[127] Neither one of the two should grant the permission if the other is reluctant to allow the association between the novices and the professed.

When the novitiate is established as part of a religious house, its segregation from the rest of the community does not set the novitiate apart as a religious community juridically independent and distinct from the remainder of the community. Still, this segregation is the basis for the relative autonomy and independence of the novitiate.[128] Moreover, this relative independence is sufficient to warrant the reservation of the Blessed Sacrament in a chapel or oratory set aside for the use of the novices, even if there is another oratory or church used by the community at large, the novices included, for the community acts of devotion.[129]

3. Separation of the Lay Novices

Canon 564, § 2, prescribes that a separate place shall be assigned to the lay novices. It does not state whether this is to be within or outside the novitiate. In the Constitution of Clement VIII it was stated that the dormitory of the lay novices was to be separate as much as possible from the *novitiate* of the choir novices.[130] Yet, despite this separation the lay novices were still subject to the same Novice Master as were the choir novices. In Cardinal Gasparri's (1852-1934) footnotes to canon 564 no reference is given to this section of the Clementine Constitution. However, the separation of the lay novices as required by the Code seems to include not only their rooms or dormitory, as the case may be, but also the place for their recreation, their lecture hall, and so on, though it is not

[127] "Commentarium Codicis"—*CpRM,* XXIV (1943), 205-206.

[128] Cf. canon 561, § 1.

[129] Creusen-Garesché-Ellis, *Religious Men and Women in the Code,* p. 156; Larraona, "Commentarium Codicis"—*CpRM,* XXIV (1943), 204. This opinion is supported by an official interpretation of canon 1267 given by the Pontifical Commission for the Interpretation of the Code, June 2-3, 1918—*AAS,* X (1918), 346-347.

[130] Clemens VIII, const. *"Cum ad regularem,"* 19 mart. 1603, § 15—*Fontes,* n. 189.

demanded that these be outside the novitiate proper.[131] Indeed, the Code supposes that all the novices will be trained in one novitiate under the same Master.[132]

Commenting on the second section of canon 564, Larraona says that it seems to be the mind of the law that communication between the choir and the lay novices generally be forbidden.[133] On the other hand, Creusen maintains that a rather frequent communication between the two classes of novices is permissible, and indeed helpful is promoting humility and charity.[134]

Vermeersch-Creusen [135] and Beste [136] say that the law of separation from the professed as regards the lay novices is more lenient than that for the choir novices. This separation is sufficiently achieved if they have their own place at table, in the dormitory, and at recreation. Thus these authors seem to imply that communication between the lay novices and the professed members of the community is not as strictly forbidden as it is in regard to the choir novices. Cocchi expressly says that the law requiring the separation of the lay novices from the professed lay brothers is somewhat mitigated.[137]

This latter interpretation seems, to the present writer, to be the more tenable one. For although the law in forbidding communication between the novices and the professed religious makes no distinction between the two classes of novices,[138] still, in requiring that the lay novices be assigned their own separate places in the novitiate, it seems to imply a mitigation of the rule established by the first part of canon 564. The authors cited above merely state this fact more or less clearly. They assign no further reason for their opinion. However, it seems that a valid reason can be drawn from the law as expressed in canon 565, § 3.

[131] Cf. Larraona, "Commentarium Codicis"—*CpRM,* XXIV (1943), 207.

[132] Schaefer, *De Religiosis,* p. 534.

[133] "Commentarium Codicis"—*CpRM,* XXIV (1943), 208.

[134] Creusen-Garesché-Ellis, *Religious Men and Women in the Code,* p. 156.

[135] *Epitome,* I, n. 664.

[136] *Introductio in Codicem,* p. 376.

[137] *Commentarium,* Lib. II, *De Personis,* pars II, 144.

[138] Canon 564, § 1.

In this canon the law states that the novices are forbidden during the year of novitiate to engage in hearing confessions, in preaching, or in the external works of the religious Institute. Obviously the first two of these prohibitions apply only to novices who are priests. Similarly the novices are forbidden to engage in the formal study of literature, of the sciences and of the arts. Finally, the law states that the lay novices may be permitted to perform such duties as are reserved to the professed lay brothers, provided that they are performed within the religious house itself, and on the condition that these duties do not interfere with the exercises of the novitiate which the lay novices are to perform. However, in performing these functions the lay novices are not to be the chief officials in charge of the tasks concerned.[139]

This last part of the canon is important. For it is thereby implied that the lay novices must work under the direction of and in conjunction with those professed lay brothers who are the primary officials in charge of the various tasks performed by them. This is allowed to the lay novices, since it is part of their training and probation. It is often necessary that they be engaged in these tasks, since many of them require a certain amount of skill and practice before they are mastered. Hence, if the lay novices are to become useful lay brothers in the community, they must have at least a rudimentary training in the various tasks they will be expected to perform in the monastery or religious house. Yet, since their spiritual formation is the main purpose of the novitiate, the lay novices are not to be so entirely preoccupied with the performance of the duties of the lay brothers as to omit any of the spiritual exercises of the novitiate, and thus risk achieving the proper religious training and spiritual formation they are bound to acquire.

It follows from this that the lay novices will necessarily have to mingle and communicate with the professed lay brothers. Hence, in view of this necessity, the law refrains from prohibiting their communication with the professed religious in the same way that it does prohibit it in regard to the choir novices.

[139] Canon 565, § 3.

D. *Profession in Articulo Mortis*

1. Historical Notes

The privilege of profession *in articulo mortis* was first granted by Pius V (1566-1572) to the nuns of the Dominican Order.[140] Prior to this concession such a privilege was not even mentioned by canonists, and Pius V seems therefore to have been the author of both the idea and the granted privilege of profession *in articulo mortis*.[141]

Most of the authors held that this privilege was participated in by novices of both sexes of any religious Institute which communicated in the privileges of the Dominican Order.[142] Not all the authors admitted this however.[143] Piatus (J. J. Loiseaux, 1815-1904) cited [144] Dominicus Ursaya (fl. 1730-1736) and Bartholomaeus de Vecchis [145] as holding that the privilege granted by Pius V was abrogated by reason of the Constitution *In tanta,* issued on March 1, 1573, by Gregory XIII (1572-1585) [146] and likewise of the Constitution *Romanus Pontifex,* issued on May 23, 1606, by Paul V (1605-1621).[147] Still Piatus maintained that it was the common opinion of the authors that Pius V's Constitution was still in force. For Gregory XIII did not revoke all the acts of Pius V granted in favor of

[140] Const. *"Summi Sacerdotii,"* 23 aug. 1570—*Bull. Rom.*, VII, 849-851. For a historical summary of this privilege cf. Hofmeister, *"Professio religiosa in articulo mortis* unter dem neuen Recht"—*TPQ,* LXXIV (1921), 493-500.

[141] *Analecta Ecclesiastica* (Romae, 1893-1911), II (1894), 498; De Langogne, "De la profession religieuse anticipée *in articulo mortis*"—*Le Canoniste Contemporain* (Paris, 1878-1922), XVIII (1895), 2.

[142] Cf. Schmalzgrueber, *Jus Ecclesiasticum Universum,* lib. III, tit. XXXI, n. 48; Reiffenstuel, *Jus Canonicum Universum,* lib. III, tit. XXXI, nn. 182, 183; Donatus, *Rerum Regularium Praxis Resolutoria,* tom. III, tract. XI, q. 10; Wernz-Vidal, *Ius Canonicum,* III, n. 296.

[143] Cf. *Le Canoniste Contemporain,* XVIII (1895), 3.

[144] *Praelectiones Juris Regularis,* I, 101, 102.

[145] A Cistercian, and more generally known as Bartholomaeus a S. Fausto or also Bartholomaeus de Bec (1571-1636).

[146] § 6—*Bull. Rom.*, VIII, 39.

[147] §§ 8, 19—*Bull. Rom.*, XI, 318.

regulars, but only those which he himself expressly designated. The Constitution *Summi Sacerdotii,* by means of which Pius V granted the privilege of profession *in articulo mortis,* was not mentioned among those of his Constitutions which Gregory XIII revoked. Nor was the privilege revoked by the Constitution of Paul V. This Constitution, it is true, recalled all *indulgences* granted to regulars, and stated clearly which ones the Pope thenceforth granted them. It is likewise true that certain indulgences were connected with the act of profession *in articulo mortis.* Yet the majority of the authors, according to Piatus, maintained that the *privilege itself* had not been revoked by this act of Paul V.

To remove all doubt in this matter and to settle any dispute as to which religious groups enjoyed the privilege, Pius X in 1912 extended to all religious Orders, Congregations and Societies, and to all monasteries and convents of religious of both sexes, and likewise to Institutes which followed the common life after the manner of religious but without vows, the privilege of allowing a novice to make his profession, consecration, or promise according to his proper constitutions, if he should be in danger of death.[148] This decree settled not only the dispute as to which religious groups enjoyed the privilege, but likewise the question that had been raised by some few authors, namely, whether or not the original grant of Pius V had ever been revoked. For the decree declared that the privilege had been enjoyed by those religious Institutes which communicated in the privileges of the Dominican Order. It likewise stated that some other religious Institutes had also obtained the privilege by special grant from the Holy See, or had incorporated it into their constitutions, which in turn had been approved by the Holy See.[149]

Concern over the existence of this privilege again arose when it was discovered that nowhere in the Code was *professio in articulo mortis* mentioned. Some canonists maintained that the decree

[148] S.C. de Religiosis, decr. "*Spirituali consolationi,*" 10 sept. 1912—*AAS,* IV (1912), 589-590.

[149] S.C. de Religiosis, decr. "*Spirituali consolationi,*" 10 sept. 1912—*AAS,* IV (1912), 589.

Spirituali consolationi had changed the character of the concession from that of a privilege to that of a general law. Hence, as a general law, since it was neither explicitly nor implicitly mentioned in the Code, it had lost its force according to the principles of canon 6, 2°. Moreover, the concession was useless, according to the argument proposed by these authors, for the law stated that novices shared in all the spiritual privileges granted to the Institute in which they were novices. Accordingly, in case of death a novice would receive the same suffrages as would a deceased professed religious.[150]

Other canonists argued that it was not at all clear that the legal character of the concession had been changed. Rather, the privilege had simply been made universal by the decree *Spirituali consolationi,* and had thus become a general privilege, not a general law. Moreover, the concession was not useless in consequence simply of the fact that novices were entitled to the same suffrages as were the professed religious should they be overtaken by death. For a death-bed profession of vows had the effect of spiritually consoling the dying novice, and furthermore gained for him the graces and supernatural merit attached to the act of religious profession.[151]

This latter opinion seems to have been the better one juridically. But at any rate the discussion is now chiefly of historical interest. For in 1922 the Holy See settled the dispute by declaring that the decree *Spirituali consolationi* was still in force, and at the same time took occasion to specify the conditions for and the effects of profession *in articulo mortis.*[152]

2. Conditions and Effects of Death-Bed Profession

The conditions that must be present before a novice in danger of death can be admitted to profession are the following:

(1) The year of novitiate or probation must have been canonically begun. Canon 553 states that the novitiate begins with the reception of the religious habit, or in any other manner prescribed by the constitutions of an Institute. Neither the decree *Spirituali*

150 Canon 567, § 1.

151 Cf. Goyeneche, "Consultatio"—*CpR,* I (1920), 51-52.

152 S.C. de Religiosis, decr. 30 dec. 1922—*AAS,* XV (1923), 156-158.

consolationi nor that of 1922 stated that the canonical age for admission to profession was required for admission to profession *in articulo mortis*.[153]

It is true that the decree *Spirituali consolationi*[154] referred to the fact that the original grant of the privilege by Pius V did require that the dying novice be of the age required by law for a valid profession. Yet the Holy See has clearly declared which conditions are necessary for a valid use of this privilege. Among these conditions no mention whatever is made of the age ordinarily required for a valid profession. Hence it seems that a dying novice could validly and lawfully be admitted to profession even though not yet sixteen years of age, provided that the novitiate had actually been begun.

The reason for this interpretation lies in the fact that, although the effects of the privilege are still the same as they were in the original grant of Pius V,[155] the conditions for its valid use have been somewhat modified by the Holy See. The question of the required age seems to be one of these modifications. Moreover, privileges are to be understood according to the tenor of the grant, and it is just as unlawful to restrict them as it is to extend them beyond the tenor of the grant.[156] Accordingly, since the Holy See has not conditioned the use of the privilege as far as age is concerned, there is no reason why it should be so conditioned.[157]

(2) The dying novice must be admitted to profession by a competent Superior. This Superior is not only the major Superior according to the constitutions, but also the Superior who is actually governing the house of novitiate or probation. Any of these Superiors can legitimately delegate another to accept the act of profession.

Originally the decree *Spirituali consolationi* had mentioned only

[153] Sixteen years is the required age for a valid temporary profession of vows. Cf. canons 572, § 1, 1°; 573.

[154] S.C. de Religiosis, decr. "*Spirituali consolationi,*" 10 sept. 1912—*AAS,* IV (1912), 589.

[155] Wernz-Vidal, *Ius Canonicum,* III, n. 296, note 69.

[156] Canon 67.

[157] Cf. Vermeersch, "De professione novicii vel probandi in articulo mortis"—*Periodica,* XII (1923), (162); Coronata, *Institutiones,* I, n. 587, note 4.

the local Superior.[158] The decree of 1922 included also the major Superior who is the competent Superior, according to the constitutions, to admit the novices to profession. The local Superior now has a cumulative right with the major Superior to admit a dying novice to profession.[159] Still, if it can be done conveniently, the major Superior should be given the preference in admitting such a novice to profession. It should be noted too that the vote of the council or chapter is not required in allowing a dying novice to make his profession of vows.[160]

The decree does not state anything which could be interpreted as including the Novice Master among those who can admit the novice to profession. It seems perfectly clear that the Master is not competent at all in this matter, since he cannot be said to be governing the *house* of the novitiate or the monastery. He would be competent only if he had been delegated by one of the Superiors competent to admit the novice to profession, or if he were at the same time the local Superior of the house of the novitiate.[161]

Creusen [162] classes the Novice Master with the local and the major Superiors, and says that any of these or their delegates can admit the dying novice to profession. No further argument or authority is given in support of this statement. In view of the wording of the decree his doctrine seems to reflect an arbitrary statement without juridic foundation.

(3) The formula to be used in admitting a dying novice to profession is the same one that is ordinarily used at profession. However, the act of profession is to be made without any determination of the time for which the vows are binding.

As regards the effects of such a profession, if the novice dies after having been professed he obtains the same graces, indulgences and suffrages as a deceased professed religious. Moreover, he gains a plenary indulgence *in forma iubilaei.* Aside from these effects no further juridical effects follow as a result of a death-bed profession

158 *AAS,* IV (1912), 590.

159 S.C. de Religiosis, decr. 30 dec. 1922—*AAS,* XV (1923), 157.

160 Schaefer, *De Religiosis,* p. 563; Berutti, *De Religiosis,* p. 187.

161 Cf. Pejška, *Ius Canonicum Religiosorum,* p. 102.

162 Creusen-Garesché-Ellis, *Religious Men and Women in the Code,* p. 164.

of vows. Therefore, should the novice die intestate the religious Institute cannot lay claim to any of the goods or property which he may have possessed. Should he recover before the end of the canonical novitiate, then the act of profession is no longer effective, and the novice is in the same juridical condition as the other novices. Accordingly, he is free to leave the novitiate if he so wishes, and can be legitimately dismissed from it. If he remains, the novitiate must be completed and the usual act of profession made at its end. However, if the year of the novitiate had been interrupted, for example, because the novice had been hospitalized outside the novitiate, the Novice Master must take care that the time necessary to complete the year of the novitiate is supplied, if this is necessary, according to the norms of canon 556. Finally, should the same novice, having recovered from his illness, again fall dangerously ill, he may again be admitted to profession *in articulo mortis*.[163]

A dying novice may be admitted to profession even though he is outside the novitiate, for instance, if he is confined to a hospital. Presence in the novitiate is not a requisite for a death-bed profession. Still, this supposes that the novitiate has not yet been interrupted to such a degree that it must be begun over again.[164] If the novice has been outside the novitiate, even legitimately, for more than thirty days, the novitiate is then interrupted and must be begun anew before the novice can be admitted to profession validly.[165] Hence, if the novice has been outside the novitiate for over thirty days and only then is in danger of death, he could not be admitted validly to a death-bed profession of vows.

A few important points remain to be noted in connection with this privilege. Although this privilege is usually referred to as profession *in articulo mortis*, that is, profession made at the *point* of death, this is to be understood in the sense of *danger* of death.[166] For the decree *Spirituali consolationi* expressly states that novices

[163] Schaefer, *De Religiosis*, p. 564.

[164] Schaefer, *De Religiosis*, p. 563.

[165] Cf. canons 555; 556; 572, § 1, 3°.

[166] Cf. Kraemer, "De professione religiosa a novitio in mortis articulo vel periculo constituto emittenda," *Periodica*, XXXI (1942), 140-142.

may be admitted to profession if in the judgment of the doctor they are gravely ill. In the subsequent explanatory phrase the decree uses the words *in articulo mortis.*[167]

In explaining the phrase *articulus mortis,* Cappello[168] states that one is at the point of death when death is very close and morally certain and indeed almost inevitable. Accordingly, if such a condition were required before a dying novice could be admitted to profession, he could hardly be expected to enjoy that spiritual consolation together with its salutary effects which the Pope intended such a novice to enjoy. Moreover, as Cappello points out,[169] "danger of death" and "at the point of death" are here taken in the same sense.

Besides, since the dying novice is required to make his act of profession by using the formula of profession usually employed, the decree can hardly be said to be considering the case of a novice for whom death is a moral certitude. Furthermore, as the decree considers the possibility of recovery, it is difficult to see that the privilege is meant only for such novices who admittedly, and thus to all appearances also inevitably, are about to die.

Goyeneche is of the opinion, however, that the decree must be interpreted literally, and hence in his opinion the privilege may be used only in favor of a novice who is at the point of death.[170] On the other hand, Kraemer[171] not only advances the arguments outlined above, but also states that most of the authors maintain that in new sets of constitutions that are to be submitted to the Holy See for approval reference to this privilege ought to read *in periculo mortis,* rather than *in articulo mortis.* To the present writer the opinion that it suffices for the use of this privilege if the novice be

[167] S.C. de Religiosis, decr. "*Spirituali consolationi,*" 10 sept. 1912—*AAS,* IV (1912), 589.

[168] *Tractatus Canonico-Moralis de Sacramentis* (3 vols. in 5, Vol. I, 2. ed., 1928; Vol. II, pars I, *De Poenitentia,* 2. ed., 1929, Taurinorum Augustae: Marietti), I, n. 481. (Hereafter this work will be cited as *De Sacramentis.*)

[169] *Loc. cit.*

[170] "Consultatio"—*CpRM,* XXIII (1942), 20.

[171] "De professione religiosa a novitio in mortis articulo vel periculo constituto emittenda"—*Periodica,* XXXI (1942), 142.

in danger of death seems perfectly safe and well-grounded on juridical reasoning.

However, this danger of death must be the result of some grave sickness. This is quite evident from the wording of the original grant of Pius V as well as that of the decree *Spirituali consolationi*.[172] It would not suffice that the novice be in some circumstance which other than sickness entailed a danger of death. For example, if a novice had been constrained to join the armed forces and then was sent to the battle-front before thirty days had elapsed since his necessitated departure from the novitiate, he could not be allowed to avail himself of this privilege on the score that being at the battle-front he was in the danger of death. He would first have to be in danger of death from sickness or wounds.[173] However, it is not required for the validity of the profession that the physician declare the novice to be actually in danger of death. Such a declaration would ordinarily have been made in the case. Yet, if it is sufficiently clear, even without the manifested judgment of the physician, that the novice is in danger of death, he may be admitted to profession.[174]

Finally, it may be asked whether or not postulants too can partake of this privilege. The title used in the decree *Spirituali consolationi* and in that of 1922 reads: "*De professione religiosa in articulo mortis novitiis vel postulantibus permissa.*" [175] Commentators noticed this immediately, and some maintained that the privilege was extended to include dying postulants as well as novices.[176] Other com-

[172] S.C. de Religiosis, decr. "*Spirituali consolationi,*" 10 sept. 1912: "Spirituali consolationi Novitiarum sancti Dominici volens consulere, . . . S. Pius V, . . . concessit et indulsit ut quoties aliqua ex iisdem Novitiis nondum professa, de alicuius medici iudicio, ab hoc saeculo transitura conspiceretur, ipsa, . . . valeret in mortis articulo regularem professionem ante finem novitiatus emittere. . . .—*AAS,* IV (1912), 589.

[173] Cf. Goyeneche, "Consultatio"—*CpRM,* XXIII (1942), 18-19.

[174] Cf. *Analecta Ecclesiastica,* II (1894), 499: "Superior absque ullo medici forsan absentis consilio praedicti novitii vota religiosa accipere certe poterit."

[175] S.C. de Religiosis, decr. "*Spirituali consolationi,*" 10 sept. 1912—*AAS,* IV (1912), 589; decr. 30 dec. 1922—*AAS,* XV (1923), 156.

[176] Vermeersch, "De professione novitii vel probandi in articulo mortis"—*Periodica,* XII (1923), (159)—(162); Maroto, "Annotationes"—*CpR,* X (1929), 338.

mentators maintained that only in the title of these decrees were postulants mentioned, and nowhere in the body of the decrees themselves. The word *probandus,* they argued, was used as a synonym for novice, just as the phrase "year of probation" is used synonymously with "year of novitiate." [177]

The intrinsic reasons given for the latter view seemed to discount the contentions of the other commentators. Yet, despite this, Goyeneche [178] admitted that postulants could be admitted to death-bed profession. He based this conclusion on a statement made by Vermeersch that he had learned privately from a Cardinal that it was the mind of the Sacred Congregation to extend this privilege to postulants.[179] This alleged intention of the Sacred Congregation was apparently untrue. For Vermeersch ultimately changed his opinion and expressly taught that postulants were excluded from this privilege.[180] Goyeneche then reverted to his original opinion, mentioning that it was the practice of the Sacred Congregation in approving sets of new constitutions to delete from these any reference which would allow the privilege of death-bed profession to be extended to postulants.[181]

Concluding this section, then, one must state that postulants may not be admitted to profession in danger of death. The arguments of those few canonists who still maintain the more liberal opinion have little intrinsic probability. Moreover, there is little extrinsic probability to the opinion, since these authors, by and large, based their opinion upon the authors who have since abandoned their former position. A final argument may be drawn from a reply given by the Sacred Congregation of Religious and quoted by Bastien (1866-1940).[182] This reply, according to this author, was given on

[177] Goyeneche, "Annotationes"—*CpR,* IV (1923), 262; "Consultatio"—*CpR,* V (1924), 165-166; Anon., "Dying Postulants Cannot Be Admitted to Profession," *The American Ecclesiastical Review* (Philadelphia, 1889-1943; Washington, 1944—), C (1939), 447-452. (Hereafter this periodical will be cited as *AER.*)

[178] "Consultatio"—*CpR,* V (1924), 166.

[179] *Periodica,* XII (1923), (161).

[180] Vermeersch-Creusen, *Epitome,* I (5. ed., 1933), n. 720.

[181] "Consultatio"—*CpR,* XIII (1932), 39-40.

[182] *Directoire Canonique,* p. 332.

March 28, 1925, and confirmed by Pius XI on August 5 of the same year. The gist of it was that postulants could not be included among those for whom the privilege of profession in danger of death had been granted. However, this reply of the Sacred Congregation did not appear in the *Acta Apostolicae Sedis,* nor, apparently, has it ever been published officially elsewhere.

CHAPTER V

THE NOVICE MASTER AND THE INTERNAL FORUM

ARTICLE 1. MANIFESTATION OF CONSCIENCE

A. The Practice of Manifestation of Conscience

FROM the earliest beginnings of cenobitic life Christians who were striving for perfection sought guidance in spiritual matters from more mature men skilled in the ways of perfection.[1] In monasteries it was usually the Superior who directed the subjects in the spiritual life. They approached him in their doubts and anxieties, yet without any obligation of doing so. This practice was first introduced into a religious rule as an obligation by St. Ignatius Loyola (1491-1556). The constitutions of the Society on this matter were subsequently more accurately defined by the General Chapters, particularly by one that was held in 1599 under Claudius Aquaviva during his incumbency as Superior General of the Order (1581-1615).[2]

Many other religious Institutes followed the example of the Jesuits in prescribing a manifestation of conscience for all the members.[3] This obtained not only in communities of men, both clerical and lay, but also, in law or in fact, in most of the communities of women religious as well, where it was often rigorously enforced.[4] The Clementine Constitution did not use the terms "manifestation of conscience," but it did prescribe "a daily opening of the interior

[1] Suarez, *De Religione,* tract. X, lib. X, cap. VI, nn. 4-6; Voltas, "De aperienda, directionis causa, superioribus conscientia"—*CpR,* I (1920), 87.

[2] Biederlack-Führich, *De Religiosis,* pp. 93-94.

[3] Battandier, *Guide canonique,* p. 261; Biederlack-Führich, *De Religiosis,* p. 94.

[4] Chelodi-Ciprotti, *Ius Canonicum de Personis,* p. 408; De Langogne: "Le nouveau décret de la S.C. des Évêques et Réguliers et l'ingérence des supérieurs et supérieures dans le for de la conscience"—*Le Canoniste Contemporain,* XIV (1891), 73.

movements of the heart and a manifestation of temptations," which the novices were to make to the Novice Master.[5]

This account of conscience has been defined by Suarez as "a manifestation of the state of one's conscience, which a subject makes to his Superior, that he may be intimately known by him, both in his conduct and in his affections or inclinations."[6] Schaefer defines it as a disclosure of the state of one's soul made outside of confession concerning those things which relate to one's virtues and vices. It includes therefore a disclosure of one's inclinations, temptations, passions and affections. Its purpose is to obtain counsel in doubts and difficulties in order to progress more surely along the way of perfection.[7]

This practice differs from the mere paternal inquiry or *colloquium* observed in many communities. This latter practice is indeed concerned with the private good of the subject, but it treats only with external matters, not with a complete manifestation of one's conscience.[8] Similarly, it differs from the public accusation of external faults against the rule, and from the practice observed in many novitiates of a mutual accusation of faults made by the novices themselves.[9] As regards the latter practice, however, the Novice Master must exercise vigilance in order that only faults against external discipline, such as transgressions of the precepts of the rule and of the constitutions, be made known. There should never be any accusations of internal faults, much less of sins.

The practice of manifesting one's conscience to the Superior obviously can be of great usefulness. Yet, the direction of souls is a difficult art which demands great prudence and an adequate knowledge of theology. Abuses can readily arise, therefore, particularly when the Superior is not a priest, and most of all when

[5] Clemens VIII, const. *"Cum ad regularem,"* 19 mart. 1603, § 9—*Fontes,* n. 189.

[6] *De Religione,* tract. X, lib. X, cap. VI, n. 2.

[7] *De Religiosis,* pp. 400-401.

[8] Wernz-Vidal, *Ius Canonicum,* III, n. 211; Raus, *Institutiones Canonicae,* p. 285.

[9] De Meester, *Compendium J.C.,* II, 420; Goyeneche, "Consultatio"—*CpR,* XI (1930), 438.

it is a question of a woman religious unskilled in theology.[10] Actually abuses did arise with the result that liberty of conscience was invaded and lay religious superiors trespassed upon the sphere reserved to the confessor. Hence the Sacred Congregation of Bishops and Regulars grew concerned and took steps to combat all such abuses. During the latter half of the nineteenth century it constantly deleted from constitutions submitted to it for approval all references to this matter.[11]

Indeed, in 1860 alone the Sacred Congregation disapproved of at least seven sets of constitutions submitted to it, all of which purported to require the practice of manifestation of conscience *as an obligation*.[12] In one instance the Sacred Congregation refused to allow the practice of the manifestation of conscience because it resembled sacramental confession too much and deserved to be censured as a false mysticism.[13]

At that time, however, nothing was done to correct the constitutions of Institutes already approved if they required the practice of the manifestation of conscience as an obligation. Such Institutes were at liberty therefore to continue the practice according to their approved constitutions.[14] But before long the Holy See attended to this matter when it issued the decree *Quemadmodum*,[15] its crowning effort to eradicate the abuses connected with the practice of the manifestation of conscience.

[10] Wernz-Vidal, *Ius Canonicum*, III, n. 212.

[11] Bastien, *Directoire Canonique*, p. 140; Sebastianelli, *Praelectiones Juris Canonici* (2. ed., 3 vols., Romae, 1905-1906), I, 399-400; Battandier, *Guide canonique*, p. 261.

[12] *AJP*, V (1861), 509; 926; 1052-1056. The language of the animadversions in almost every instance was the same: "In praesens manifestatio conscientiae restringitur quoad publicas transgressiones regulae, et ad progressum in virtutibus et quidem non obligatorie, sed facultative."—*AJP*, VI (1861), 1052.

[13] "Cela ressemble trop à la confession sacramentelle, et pourrait étre censurè comme un faux mysticisme."—*AJP*, IV (1860), 1325.

[14] Valuy, *Le gouvernement des communautés religieuses* (2. ed., Paris, 1866), p. 618.

[15] S.C. Ep. et Reg., decr. "*Quemadmodum*," 17 dec. 1890—*Fontes*, n. 2017.

B. Application of the Decree Quemadmodum to the Novice Master

The decree *Quemadmodum*, published at the command of Leo XIII (1878-1903), applied only to lay religious Institutes, but included all such Institutes both of men and of women. It dealt with three points: the suppression of the *obligation* of the manifestation of conscience, the refusal by Superiors to give a subject permission for an extraordinary confessor,[16] and the refusal of Holy Communion to subjects by Superiors. The decree forbade Superiors to deny an extraordinary confessor to their subjects if the latter requested one for the sake of conscience. Superiors were not to inquire in any way into the subject's reason for the request.[17] The decree likewise ordered that it belonged solely to the ordinary or the extraordinary confessor to grant or to withhold permission to receive Holy Communion, and stated that the religious Superiors had no authority in this matter.[18]

The strongest language was used in the decree in the abolition of the practice of the manifestation of conscience as an obligation on the part of lay religious. Even though the constitutions of the Institute might have been approved by the Holy See in the most solemn manner, still by this decree the Holy Father abrogated everything connected with the intimate manifestation of one's conscience as an obligation imposed by the constitutions of any religious Institute or Society of women, whether of solemn or of simple vows, and of all lay Institutes of men. The higher Superiors of all such Institutes, Congregations and Societies were further commanded to delete completely from their constitutions, directories and manuals any statute or prescription that required a manifestation of conscience. Likewise all usages and customs, even immemorial customs, in this matter were to be stopped.[19]

The Superiors and Superioresses of the Institutes concerned, re-

[16] Cf. Conc. Trident., sess. XXV, *de regularibus*, c. 10; Benedictus XIV, const. "*Pastoralis curae*," 5 aug. 1748, §§ 2, 3—*Fontes*, n. 388.

[17] S.C. Ep. et Reg., decr. "*Quemadmodum*," 17 dec. 1890, n. 4—*Fontes*, n. 2017.

[18] *Ibid.*, n. 5—*Fontes*, n. 2017.

[19] *Ibid.*, n. 1—*Fontes*, n. 2017.

gardless of their position and eminence, were therefore absolutely forbidden to induce their subjects whether directly or indirectly, by precept or counsel, by fear or by threats, to make a manifestation of conscience to themselves. Moreover, the subjects were obliged to denounce to their major Superiors any lower Superior who had offended against this law. If the major Superior or Superioress was guilty, he or she was to be denounced to the Sacred Congregation of Bishops and Regulars.[20]

The decree however did not forbid the subjects from freely disclosing the state of their souls to their Superiors for the sake of obtaining counsel and guidance in their doubts and anxieties, and in order to make progress in virtue.[21] Nor were such practices as "the chapter of faults" forbidden, namely, a public and open acknowledgment of external faults against the religious rule and constitutions.[22] Finally, the decree required that a translation of its prescriptions in the vernacular be inserted in the constitutions of the Institutes to which it applied, and that this translation be read before the community of each religious house at least once a year.[23]

In abolishing this practice the Holy See made no exceptions. Even though the practice may have been followed without any abuses in a given religious Institute, still this offered no excuse for retaining the practice as an obligation imposed by the constitutions of the Institute.[24] This decree was thought so important that the Sacred Congregation of Religious in 1910 commanded all ordinaries to see to it that it, and others of similarly grave import to religious, again be brought to the attention of Religious Families and Institutes, even to those of diocesan approval.[25]

There naturally arises the question whether or not the Master and Mistress of Novices were bound by the decree *Quemadmodum*. Arguing from intrinsic reasons, one must clearly conclude that they

[20] *Ibid.*, n. 2—*Fontes*, n. 2017.

[21] *Ibid.*, n. 3—*Fontes*, n. 2017.

[22] Cf. *AER*, XX (1899), 420-421.

[23] S.C. de Rel., decr. *"Quemadmodum,"* 17 dec. 1890, n. 8—*Fontes*, n. 2017.

[24] De Langogne: "Le nouveau décret de la S. C. des Évêques et Réguliers et l'ingérence des supérieurs et supérieures dans le for de la conscience."—*Le Canoniste Contemporain*, XIV (1891), 110.

[25] S.C. de Religiosis, decr. 3 iul. 1910—*Fontes*, n. 4404.

were bound. For if Superiors were forbidden to oblige their professed subjects to make the manifestation of conscience, then *a fortiori* they could not oblige novices and postulants. It seems too that Superiors in the broad sense, Masters and Mistresses of Novices included, were comprised under this prohibition as well as Superiors in the strict sense of the term.[26] The purpose of the Holy See in issuing this decree was to eradicate an abuse from the entire religious life. Hence it could hardly tolerate the practice in the novitiate. Moreover, then as now, in things favorable novices were considered true religious in matters that could apply to them. Surely this decree was applicable to them, since for them, too, it implied a matter of favor inasmuch as it was issued to safeguard the right of freedom of conscience.

Now, since this matter of the application of the decree to the Novice Master will have an important bearing on what will be said later concerning the application of canon 530, § 1, to the Master, it will be necessary to consider the opinions of some of the authors who commented on the decree of Leo XIII.

Vermeersch attests that very many, if not most of the authors, considered that the Novice Master was included in the word *Superiores* as used in the decree *Quemadmodum*.[27] However, at first he himself argued that only Superiors in the strict sense of the term were included under the prohibition. Yet, he admitted that most of the authors held the opposite opinion. Vermeersch argued that novices were not religious in the strict sense, and that Novice Masters and Mistresses would be hampered in their task of forming religious if they were bound by the decree. As a supplementary argument he added that he had knowledge of a Cardinal Protector of a certain religious Congregation who had said that the decree did not apply to novices.

But in a subsequent edition of his work Vermeersch, quoting article 79 of the *Normae* of 1901,[28] changed his former opinion, and

[26] Bastien, *Directoire Canonique*, p. 142.

[27] *De Religiosis Institutis et Personis* (2. ed., 2 vols., Romae, 1907), I, 325.

[28] "Non tenentur tamen suae conscientiae statum manifestum facere magistrae novitiarum, nec moderatricibus Instituti, neque ipsis anteactae vitae suae rationem reddere, neque ad hoc induci possunt (Decr. *Quemadmodum*)."

expressly stated that it appeared no longer doubtful that novices also were contemplated in the decree *Quemadmodum*.[29] It is perfectly clear that in saying this Vermeersch was speaking of the novices' relation to the Master, and not only of their relation to the Superiors. For in the first edition of his work he had expressly stated that novices did not come under the decree, for the precise reason that the Novice Master could hardly exercise his office without anxiety if he were bound by the law.[30]

In the editions of their commentaries published after the promulgation of the decree *Quemadmodum*, some authors, such as Wernz (1842-1914) and De Angelis (1824-1881) seem not to have considered the question of manifestation of conscience at all. Others, such as Vives (1854-1913) and Santi (1830-1885) did little more than repeat the decree itself. But with the sole exception of Vermeersch in the earlier editions of his work, none were found who expressly stated that the Novice Master was not bound by the decree. On the other hand, there were several authors who at least implied that the Master was bound by the prescriptions of the decree concerning the manifestation of conscience.

Lanslots (1859-1931) in quoting article 79 of the *Normae*, stated that the decree *Quemadmodum* applied to novices and postulants alike. It seems clear from the context that he was speaking of their relation to the Novice Master, and not only of their relation to the major or local Superiors.[31]

Arndt (1851-1925) in treating of the decree in question, drew several deductions from it.[32] Among these he remarked on the obligation which religious Superioresses had of keeping the direction which they give their subjects within the bounds set by the Holy See. Then, to demonstrate how wide these bounds were, he furnished a quotation from the constitutions of the Gray Sisters approved by the

[29] "Itaque non iam ambigendum videtur, contra ac dicebamus, ed. 1, t. 1, n. 492, novicios comprehendi decreto *Quemadmodum*."—*De Religiosis Institutis et Personis* (4. ed., 1909), II, p. (148).

[30] *De Religiosis Institutis et Personis* (ed. 1902), I, n. 492 c.

[31] *Handbook of Canon Law for Congregations of Women under Simple Vows* (5. ed., New York: Pustet, 1911), p. 55.

[32] *Die kirchlichen Rechtsbestimmungen für die Frauen-Congregationen* (Mainz, 1901), pp. 208-209.

Holy See in 1898. This quotation in turn referred not to Superioresses in the strict sense, but to Novice Mistresses, clearly indicating thereby, so it appears, that the author regarded Novice Masters and Mistresses included in the term "superior" as used in the decree *Quemadmodum.*[33]

Similarly, Piatus in treating of article 79 of the *Normae,* maintained that, since reference was there made to the decree *Quemadmodum,* article 79 was to be applied only to lay Institutes whose members professed simple vows.[34] From the context he apparently understood Novice Masters, in lay Institutes at least, to be bound by the decree *Quemadmodum,* at least in the light of the subsequent jurisprudence of the Sacred Congregation of Bishops and Regulars. Later, in treating of the questions which a religious Superior could put to a subject without offending against the prescriptions of the decree, to show how far this right of the Superior extended in this matter, he quoted the same passage from the constitutions of the Gray Sisters, as did Arndt.[35] It seems therefore that Piatus was implying that he too regarded the Novice Master bound by the decree *Quemadmodum.*

In a short work, written in 1901, the Jesuit Father Franco, in dealing with some of the abuses corrected by the decree *Quemadmodum,* spoke simultaneously of Superioresses and Novice Mistresses, thereby implying that both alike were bound by the prescriptions of the decree concerning the manifestation of conscience.[36]

[33] "Die Leitung der Oberin hat sich in den durch den heiligen Stuhl angegebenen Grenzen zu halten. Wie weit dieselben gesteckt sind, lässt sic aus den im Jahre 1898 vom heiligen Stuhle approbirten Constitutionen der Grauen Schwestern ersehen, in denen es heisst: (Theil II, Kap. 18, Von der Novizenmeisterin, n. 6): 'Die Novizenmeisterin frage ihre Novizinnen allmonatlich einmal, wie sie sich bei den Uebungen der Gebete, Betrachtungen, Tugenden und Selbstverleugnungen gehalten haben und die Vollkommenheit erstreben. Nachdem sie alles geprüft, ermuntere und entflamme sie dieselben zu höheren Fortschritten.' "—Arndt, *op. cit., loc. cit.*

[34] *Praelectiones Juris Regularis,* I, 122-123.

[35] *Praelectiones Juris Regularis,* I, 521-522.

[36] *Direction de Conscience. Lettre a une Supérieure Religieuse* (transl. A. E. Gautier, 4. ed., Paris: Téqui, 1936), pp. 42-43. Meynard, Lehmkuhl and Adigard published similar brief commentaries on the decree of 1890, but the present author was unable to unearth them.

De Langogne [37] in his commentary on the decree *Quemadmodum* remarked that he understood certain persons to consider novitiates and scholasticates as not subject to the decree. He, however, dismissed such an interpretation, arguing that the very text of the decree and the object which the Holy See wished to attain absolutely excluded such a limitation. The law, he maintained, was just as likely, and even more so, to have good results in the novitiates and scholasticates as in the houses of the professed religious.

De Langogne did not say expressly that the Novice Master was bound by the decree. But in light of the fact that the Master was the sole superior of the novitiate and that he alone had full charge of directing and forming the novices in the religious life, it seems reasonable to suppose that De Langogne did regard the Novice Master included under the prohibition of demanding in any way whatsoever a manifestation of conscience from those subject to him.

Finally, Bastien [38] maintained that the decree *Quemadmodum* applied both to novices and to postulants, and that the Novice Master as well as Superiors in the strict sense were forbidden to demand of them a manifestation of conscience.

C. *Application of Canon 530 to the Novice Master*

The prohibitions of the decree *Quemadmodum* are substantially repeated in canon 530 of the Code of Canon Law. There are, however, a few important differences between the two laws. In the first place, the decree *Quemadmodum* applied only to lay religious Institutes, whereas the present law strictly forbids all religious Superiors, even those of clerical exempt religious Institutes, to induce in any way whatsoever persons subject to them to make a manifestation of conscience to them.[39] A second difference consists in this that the present law does not oblige the subjects to denounce a Superior who offends against the law.[40] Yet, there may be at times an

[37] "Le nouveau décret de la S.C. des Évêques et Réguliers et l'ingérence des supérieurs et supérieures dans le for de la conscience."—*Le Canoniste Contemporain,* XIV (1891), 254.

[38] *Directoire Canonique* (ed. 1904), pp. 58; 226.

[39] Canon 530, § 1.

[40] Berutti, *De Religiosis,* p. 108; Vermeersch-Creusen, *Epitome,* I, n. 599.

obligation in charity, even a grave obligation, to denounce a Superior who transgresses this law, especially if the offence is frequently committed. Usually, however, this obligation would rest upon the assistants and counsellors of the Superior concerned.[41]

In interpreting canon 530, § 1, the vast majority of the commentators maintains that the word *superiores* as used in that canon must be interpreted strictly. Hence the Novice Master is not included in the letter of the law which prohibits religious Superiors to induce those persons who are subject to them to make an intimate manifestation of conscience to them. Wernz-Vidal rightly state that this is the common opinion of the authors.[42]

Most of these authors, however, argue that, although the Novice Master is not bound by the letter of the law, he is bound by its spirit inasmuch as he is forbidden to force or constrain the novices subject to him to manifest the state of their consciences to him. They explain this by saying that the Master is forbidden to force or constrain the novices, but is not forbidden to commend and even urge the practice. This is allowed to him since he is not a Superior in the strict sense.[43]

Goyeneche reasons [44] that since the Novice Master is not a religious Superior in the strict sense he can commend the practice to the novices. Moreover, he continues, the Master's relation to the novices is not identical with that of the Superior to his subjects. Hence, this identity being lacking, there is no reason to apply the letter of the law to the Novice Master. Finally, since the position

[41] Creusen-Garesché-Ellis, *Religious Men and Women in the Code,* p. 98; Bastien, *Directoire Canonique* (4. ed., 1933), p. 142.

[42] *Ius Canonicum,* III, n. 213; cf. Schaefer, *De Religiosis,* p. 402; Fanfani, *De Iure Religiosorum,* n. 132; Blat, *Ius de Religiosis,* p. 239; Beste, *Introductio in Codicem,* p. 349; Vermeersch-Creusen, *Epitome,* I, n. 599; Ferreres, *Institutiones Canonicae* (2. ed., 2 vols., Barcinone, 1920), I, 382; Papi, *Religious in Church Law* (New York: Kenedy, 1924), p. 160.

[43] Goyeneche, "Consultatio"—*CpRM,* XX (1939), 18; Voltas, "De aperienda, directionis causa, superioribus conscientia"—*CpR,* I (1920), 150-151; Schaefer, *De Religiosis,* pp. 402; 535; Wernz-Vidal, *Ius Canonicum,* III, n. 213; Vito, *De Religiosis,* p. 206; Fanfani, *De Iure Religiosorum,* n. 208; Larraona, "Commentarium Codicis"—*CpR,* XII (1931), 124-130.

[44] "Consultatio"—*CpR,* V (1924), 160-161.

of the Master is a special one inasmuch as his whole office is concerned with the spiritual formation of the novices, to such an extent even that the external government of the novitiate as such is placed exclusively under his authority, there is no reason to forbid him to commend and counsel this practice. For without it, says Goyeneche, the objective of the novitiate, namely the spiritual formation of the novices, can hardly be accomplished.

These authors quite generally say that not only must the Master refrain from demanding this practice of the novices, but also he must not show himself adverse to those novices who do not freely make this manifestation of conscience to him. Any manifestation of conscience made by a novice must be entirely free and spontaneous on his part. Therefore, in commending the practice, the Master must abstain from praising those who practice it and from exaggerating the dangers to which those who do not practice it expose themselves.[45] The novices on their part have no obligation to reveal the state of their conscience to the Master.[46] Finally, these authors correctly say that the obligation which the Master has of not forcing a novice to make a manifestation of conscience to him is a grave obligation, though of course there is room for slightness of matter.[47]

There are, however, a few commentators who hold that the Master is bound not only by the spirit of the law of canon 530, § 1, but likewise by the letter of the law.[48]

Bastien readily admits that the Novice Master is not a religious Superior in the strict sense. Hence, if canon 530, § 1, is considered alone, it must be admitted that the Novice Master is not bound by the letter of the law. But, he argues, since canon 530, § 1, is almost literally the same as section 2 of the decree *Quemadmodum,* and since the jurisprudence of the Sacred Congregation of Bishops and Regulars and later on of the Sacred Congregation of Religious in-

[45] Wernz-Vidal, *Ius Canonicum,* III, n. 213; Schaefer, *De Religiosis,* pp. 402-403; Fanfani, *De Iure Religiosorum,* n. 208.

[46] Goyeneche, "Consultatio"—*CpRM,* XVIII (1937), 93.

[47] Schaefer, *De Religiosis,* p. 402; Larraona, "Commentarium Codicis"—*CpR,* XII (1931), 127.

[48] Bastien, *Directoire Canonique* (4. ed., 1933), pp. 141-142; Berutti, *De Religiosis,* p. 109; Chelodi-Ciprotti, *Ius Canonicum de Personis,* p. 408.

terpreted the words of the decree as applying, not only to Superiors in the strict sense, but also to Masters and Mistresses of Novices, it follows that these latter are bound by the letter of the law of canon 530, § 1, even though they are not Superiors in the strict sense of the term.

Berutti argues that, just as Religious Superiors are forbidden habitually to hear the confessions of their subjects without a grave cause [49] lest difficulties and dangers in the external government of the community arise because of knowledge gained through the confessional, so for the same reason Superiors are forbidden to induce their subjects to make a manifestation of conscience to them. Novice Masters, on the other hand, are forbidden by canon 891 to hear the confessions of novices subject to them even more strictly than are religious Superiors forbidden to hear the confessions of their subjects. Therefore canon 530 should be applied just as strictly, and even more so, to Novice Masters. Berutti admits that the Novice Master certainly is not a religious Superior in the strict sense. But he maintains that canon 530, § 1, is established for all religious Superiors in relation to those persons who are subject to them. Hence there is no need to exclude the Novice Master. Indeed he is understood to be included in the law.

Chelodi-Ciprotti's opinion is that the Novice Master is included in the law because of the law's purpose. It should be noted here that many of the commentators who hold the common view cite Jansen [50] among those authors who hold that the Novice Master is bound by the letter of the law of canon 530. This identification of Jansen's doctrine with the minority view cannot any longer be rightfully maintained, for in a later edition of his work this author adopted the common view, but without giving any reason for his change of opinion.[51]

Despite the fact that the greater number of the authors is of the opinion that the Novice Master is not bound by the letter of the law which forbids religious Superiors to induce their subjects

[49] Canon 518, § 2.

[50] *Ordensrecht* (2. ed., 1920), p. 148.

[51] "Dieses Verbot [viz. of canon 530, § 1] bezieht sich nicht auf den Novizenmeister"—*Ordensrecht* (3. ed., 1931), p. 205.

to make a manifestation of conscience to them, the contrary opinion seems to the present writer to be the only correct one. This opinion is based on the identity of the present law with the old law as found in the decree *Quemadmodum*.

The commentators who follow the common opinion insist that the word *superiores* of canon 530, § 1, must be interpreted strictly. Hence the Novice Master does not come under its prohibition. Creusen rightly says that the definitions of the Code ought to be applied strictly, unless there is proof to the contrary. Otherwise there is danger of falling into arbitrary judgments.[52] But he and most of the authors consulted fail to consider whether there actually exists any such proof as will warrant a wide interpretation in this case. It is the conviction of the present writer that such proof exists, so that the canon *must* be interpreted to include Novice Masters and Mistresses under the prohibition it establishes.

As has already been shown, the present law is an amplification of the law established by Leo XIII in his decree *Quemadmodum*. The chief difference between the two laws is that the present prohibition extends to all religious Institutes, whereas the decree of Leo XIII applied only to lay religious Institutes. Now, according to the principles of canon 6, 2° and 3°, laws which are derived from the earlier law, in whole or in part, *must* be interpreted according to the authority of the earlier law, and hence according to the accepted interpretation put upon the earlier law by approved authors. Only insofar as the present law is dissimilar from the earlier legislation is it to be interpreted according to its own phraseology.[53]

Now, since both the jurisprudence of the Sacred Congregation of Bishops and Regulars, as embodied in the *Normae* of 1901 and the interpretation of the commentators clearly seem to include the Novice Master among those who were bound by the decree *Quemadmodum*,

[52] Creusen-Garesché-Ellis, *Religious Men and Women in the Code*, p. 97.

[53] Canon 6, 2°—Canones qui ius vetus ex integro referunt, ex veteris iuris auctoritate, atque ideo ex receptis apud probatos auctores interpretationibus, sunt aestimandi;

3°—Canones, qui ex parte tantum cum veteri iure congruunt, qua congruunt, ex iure antiquo aestimandi sunt; qua discrepant, sunt ex sua ipsorum sententia diiudicandi.

it follows that the Novice Master must likewise be included in the term *superiores* as used in canon 530.

This conclusion seems to be the only one consistent with the principles established by canon 6, 2° and 3°, for the interpretation of those canons which are derived, in whole or in part, from the earlier law. Keeping in mind the all-important fact that the jurisprudence of the Sacred Congregations and the interpretation of the commentators both regarded the Novice Master as bound by the decree *Quemadmodum,* one is forced to conclude in the light of the principles of canon 6 that the Master is also bound by the letter of the law of canon 530, § 1. This obligation however does not arise from the decree *Quemadmodum,* but from the authority of the present law itself. Moreover, there is no need to seek for further reasons why the Novice Master is bound by canon 530, § 1, no need, for example, to appeal to the purpose of the law. The purpose of the Holy See in establishing the original law in the decree of Leo XIII may well have influenced jurisprudence and the interpretation of the commentators to consider the Novice Master bound by the decree. But the sole reason why the present writer considers the Novice Master bound by the letter of canon 530, § 1, is that of the principles established by the law itself for the interpretation of laws derived from the earlier law.

Some of the authors who hold the opposite view argue that the Novice Master would be hampered in his office of directing and forming the novices if he were bound by the letter of the law of canon 530, § 1.[54] In arguing that the formation of the novices could hardly be achieved without the practice of manifestation of conscience, these authors seem to imply that this is a supplementary argument why the Master *cannot* be bound by the prescription of canon 530, § 1.

To the present writer, this argument seems to be somewhat beside the point. For there can be no question concerning whether the Master should or should not be bound by the law, if there is legal evidence to show that he is actually bound by it. Furthermore, the contention that the formation of the novices could hardly, or only

[54] Cf. Wernz-Vidal, *Ius Canonicum,* III, n. 283, note 30; Schaefer, *De Religiosis,* p. 535.

with difficulty, be achieved unless the Master is free to urge and exhort them to make an intimate manifestation of conscience to him seems somewhat exaggerated. For, as Goyeneche and Schaefer (both of whom hold the common opinion) correctly point out, the office of the Novice Master does *not* consist in his being the principal and exclusive moderator of the consciences of the novices subject to him.[55] Indeed, there is not a single word about this in the whole section of the Code concerning the Novice Master. This fact is further confirmed by canon 891, which clearly distinguishes between the external and the internal *fora* when it forbids the Novice Master under ordinary circumstances to hear the confessions of the novices committed to his care.

There appears to be no valid reason why the spiritual formation of the novices should be thwarted if the Master is bound by the letter of the law of canon 530, § 1. Since the legislator himself has made a clear distinction between the external and internal *fora,* there is no reason why the Novice Master or Mistress could not explain the practice of manifestation of conscience and its advantages to the novices. They could then explain the law of canon 530 to the novices clearly and fully, and finally urge them to manifest the state of their conscience to their confessor or some other priest counsellor whom they can approach and in whom they have confidence.

If, as a result of this instruction, the novices approach the Novice Master himself, their act will be entirely free and unconstrained.[56] However, in such a case, Novice Mistresses and those Novice Masters who are not priests must be especially careful not to infringe upon the office of the confessor. Therefore they must not question the novice on matters pertaining to confession.[57]

Even though the novice freely and spontaneously proposes doubts and anxieties of conscience or asks advice and counsel on matters that properly belong only to confession, the Novice Mistress and those Novice Masters who are not priests should advise that the matter be taken up with the confessor, or with some other priest.

[55] Cf. Goyeneche, "Consultatio"—*CpRM* XVIII (1937), 90-91; Schaefer, *De Religiosis,* p. 535.

[56] Cf. canon 530, § 2.

[57] Fanfani, *De Iure Religiosorum,* n. 208.

Similarly, if a novice is questioned on such delicate and personal matters, he should either prudently elude answering the question, or declare openly that he prefers to discuss such matters only with his confessor.[58] This is clear from the law itself. For although it allows a voluntary and spontaneous manifestation of conscience, and even commends it and declares it expedient, still it counsels religious to make known their doubts and anxieties of conscience only to priest Superiors.[59]

It follows from this that it would be a very grave abuse for the Novice Master, even if a priest, to demand an intimate manifestation of conscience from the novices, especially since such a manifestation would almost necessarily include matters that belong only to the domain of the Sacrament of Penance. Indeed, as Creusen remarks,[60] only by one's own free agreement or by the obligation of the divine law has one man the right to ask of another such a manifestation. Moreover, lay Novice Masters would be in grave danger of misdirecting the novices because of their insufficient knowledge of ascetical, mystical and especially of moral theology. Since canon 891 forbids even Novice Masters who are priests to hear the confessions of their charges except under certain strictly determined circumstances, there is all the more reason why the Novice Master, even if a priest, cannot demand these confidences outside of confession.

On the other hand, however, it is not forbidden to the Novice Master to have periodical paternal talks with the novices, and to question them on the various aspects of the novitiate life. Such talks and questioning serve as a necessary means for enabling the Master to check the results of his teaching and direction of the novices. But, again, these questions must not be concerned with matters reserved to the confessional even though the Master may himself be a priest. Still, if the novice asks some advice of the Master, he should not deny this unless there is a really sufficient

[58] Berutti, *De Religiosis,* p. 109.

[59] Canon 530, § 2; Wernz-Vidal, *Ius Canonicum,* III, n. 213; Schaefer, *De Religiosis,* p. 404; Larraona, "Commentarium Codicis"—*CpR,* XII (1931), 129.

[60] Creusen-Garesché-Ellis, *Religious Men and Women in the Code,* pp. 97-98.

reason.[61] The novices, in turn, when questioned about the external discipline of the novitiate and about their external observance of the rules and constitutions are bound to answer truthfully.[62]

The Master may therefore question the novice on his external observance of the rule and constitutions, about the ease and difficulty he experiences in vocal and mental prayer, about the various exercises of the novitiate and the occupations of the Institute, about any difficulties he may find in leading the common life, and on similar matters. The confession of purely interior faults, of temptations, and much more of sins, must be left to the confessional. It will be the duty of the confessor, in turn, to determine whether the novice has the obligation of making known to the Master certain interior faults or difficulties which might make his remaining in the Institute difficult or harmful.[63]

Concerning the phrase "doubts and anxieties of conscience" as used in canon 530, § 2, Schaefer maintains [64] that the words must be widely interpreted, and hence refer to sins committed in the past and to cases of conscience. Larraona, on the contrary,[65] is of the opinion that they are to be strictly interpreted, and refer to cases which because of their difficulty, gravity or uncertainty demand priestly counsel and advice.

It should be noted that the Code does not forbid religious to disclose their doubts and anxieties to their Superiors who are not priests. Still, on the other hand, it does not counsel it. But it does counsel that such matters be disclosed only to Superiors who are priests. Hence it implies that when the Superior, and in the presently considered case the Novice Master, is not a priest, such doubts and

[61] Cf. Creusen-Garesché-Ellis, *Religious Men and Women in the Code,* p. 99.

[62] Berutti, *De Religiosis,* p. 109.

[63] Creusen-Garesché-Ellis, *op. cit.,* pp. 156-157; Vermeersch, *Theologiae Moralis Principia, Responsa, Consilia* (2. ed., 4 vols., Brugis: Beyaert, 1926-1928), III, n. 143.

[64] *De Religiosis,* p. 404.

[65] "Commentarium Codicis"—*CpR,* XII (1931), 130, note 431.

anxieties ought rather to be submitted to the confessor, or to some other priest counsellor.[66]

Finally, it must be remarked that in making his report on the novices to the Superiors, under no condition may the Master include in it information which he has obtained solely through a manifestation of conscience made to him by the novice.[67]

Suarez held a more liberal view concerning knowledge gained through a manifestation of conscience made outside of confession.[68] Goyeneche, however,[69] following the teaching of Wernz-Vidal,[70] restricts the liberty too freely attributed to Superiors in this matter by Suarez. Wernz-Vidal admit that knowledge obtained through a manifestation of conscience can be used provided that no harm or inconvenience to the subject, and hence no revelation of the secret, results. An example would be the action of a Superior keeping a subject from some task or duty which he knows is dangerous to the subject. But in any case the strict obligation of rigorously guarding the secret must be insisted on, so that the Master cannot manifest it even to the higher Superiors of the Institute. Nor can he use the knowledge of the secret to the harm of the subject concerned.

Vermeersch in defending this same position [71] remarked that just as a subject can positively prohibit the use of any knowledge revealed by him to the Superior, so he can also grant a degree of liberty to use it. This consent, Vermeersch contended, can even be presumed at times, but only very circumspectly and with great prudence. But, at all events, it seems clear that the Novice Master cannot use any knowledge revealed to him through a manifestation of conscience in making his report on the novices to the higher Superiors.[72]

[66] Wernz-Vidal, *Ius Canonicum,* III, n. 213; Schaefer, *De Religiosis,* p. 404; Jardi, *El Derecho de las Religiosas* (2. ed., Vich: Typografía Franciscana, 1927), p. 137.

[67] Goyeneche, "Consultatio"—*CpRM,* XVIII (1937), 95; Larraona, "Commentarium Codicis"—*CpRM,* XXIV (1943), 121.

[68] *De Religione,* tom. IV, tract. X, lib. X, cap. IV, nn. 12, 13.

[69] "Consultatio"—*CpRM,* XVIII (1937), 95.

[70] *Ius Canonicum,* III, n. 210, note 57.

[71] *De Religiosis Institutis et Personis* (1. ed., 1902), I, n. 489.

[72] Goyeneche, "Consultatio"—*CpRM,* XVIII (1937), 95.

ARTICLE 2. THE NOVICE MASTER AS CONFESSOR

A. Historical Antecedents

The present law of canon 891 in forbidding the Novice Master and his *Socius* under ordinary circumstances to hear the confessions of the novices in their care is a complete reversal of the law and practice that had existed practically up to the time of the promulgation of the Code. Before the seventeenth century it was the customary monastic practice for the Novice Master alone to be the ordinary confessor of the novices. Concerning the confessions of male *lay* religious and the novices in such Institutes, there were no special and definite regulations of the general law prior to the decree *Quemadmodum* of Leo XIII. Similarly the confessors for the novices in Institutes of women religious apparently followed the same regulations that had been established for the professed religious.[73]

The first general prescription of law on this matter for clerical religious Institutes seems to have been that of the Constitution *Cum ad regularem*. This required that the novices should confess at least least twice a month, the Novice Master alone being their ordinary confessor. It was permitted to the Superior of the monastery, however, to hear the confessions of the novices either personally or through a delegate once or twice a year, if he deemed it advisable.[74] No mention whatever was made of the *Socius* except by inference inasmuch as the office of ordinary confessor was expressly reserved to the Novice Master alone.

In 1899 the Holy Office issued a decree prohibiting the Superiors of religious communities, of seminaries and of colleges in the City of Rome from hearing the confessions of their respective subjects except in some rare cases of necessity.[75] Shortly afterwards the Holy Office explained that this decree was not intended to derogate from

[73] Cf. McCormick, *Confessors of Religious*, The Catholic University of America Canon Law Studies, n. 33 (Washington, D. C.: The Catholic University of America, 1926), pp. 45; 75-99.

[74] Clemens VIII, const. *"Cum ad regularem,"* 19 mart. 1603, §§ 9, 10—*Fontes*, n. 189.

[75] S.C.S. Off., 5 iul. 1899—*Fontes*, n. 1225.

the Apostolic Constitutions regarding religious Orders.[76] Hence, Novice Masters in religious Orders of men in Rome as elsewhere were to continue as the ordinary confessors of the novices, and the Superiors were still permitted to hear the confessions of the novices twice a year according to the prescriptions of the Clementine Constitution. Still later in the same year the Holy Office again explained that, although the religious Orders were to continue to abide by the earlier Apostolic Constitutions, religious Congregations were to follow the decree of the Holy Office of July 5, 1899.[77] As a result, Superiors in religious Congregations of men could no longer hear the confessions of the novices, except in rare cases of necessity. Therefore Novice Masters who were at the same time Superiors in a religious Congregation were forbidden to be the ordinary confessors for their novices.

Since the Novice Master was the ordinary confessor of the novices and since he was also obliged to render a report on the novices to the higher Superiors, there was always the potential danger of his confusing the internal and the external *fora* and of using knowledge gained in the confessional for the government of the community or for the making of his report to the Superiors. Actually, some authors were of the opinion that a Superior could use knowledge against a subject even when he had gained it in the confessional.[78] Following such an opinion a Novice Master could have used knowledge obtained through confession in securing the dismissal of a novice. In any case, the confusion of the two offices of Superior and Novice Master was surely capable of rendering confession odious, and thus was fraught with the danger of spiritual harm to the penitents. However, this opinion could hardly be sustained in the light of the admonition of Clement VIII, who warned religious Superiors and confessors who became Superiors to guard most diligently against

[76] S.C.S. Off., 23 aug. 1899—*Acta Sanctae Sedis* (41 vols., Romae, 1865-1908), XXXII (1899), 253. (Hereafter this collection will be cited as *ASS*).

[77] S.C.S. Off., 20 dec. 1899—*Fontes*, n. 1233; *ASS*, XXXII (1899), 504-505.

[78] Vasquez, *Commentaria ac Disputationes in tertiam partem Sancti Thomae* (4 vols., Lugduni, 1631), q. 93, art. 4, dubium VIII, nn. 5-7.

using any knowledge in the government of their communities if that knowledge had been gained in the confessional.[79]

The Holy See made its position perfectly clear later on when it condemned the proposition that a confessor could use knowledge gained in the confessional, as long as there was no danger of betrayal, in cases where the non-use of the knowledge would cause a much greater evil to the penitent than the use of the knowledge would cause.[80] There is no doubt therefore that a Novice Master could not, and cannot, legitimately use knowledge acquired through the confession of a novice.[81] This condemned opinion however differed widely from the question of merely guiding and directing a novice in the confessional and of advising him on his vocation on the basis of matter confessed. St. Raymond of Pennafort (ca. 1175-1275) advocated this latter practice as a means of supplementing one's knowledge concerning the novice already acquired in the external forum.[82] But St. Raymond allowed absolutely no use of the knowledge gained in the confessional against the penitent.[83]

A final question arises concerning the obligation of the novices to confess to the Novice Master. The law of Clement VIII apparently wished the Novice Master to be the ordinary confessor for the novices. Yet it did not expressly forbid the novices to confess to other approved confessors, unless the faculties of a given priest

[79] Clemens VIII, decr. *"Sanctissimus,"* 26 maii 1593, § 4: "Tam Superiores pro tempore existentes, quam confessarii, qui ad superioritatis gradum fuerint promoti, caveant diligentissime, ne ea notitia, quam de aliorum peccatis in confessione habuerunt, ad exteriorem gubernationem utantur."—*Fontes,* n. 177. Although this decree was issued for Regular Superiors, still it was applicable to all religious Superiors, for its purpose, viz. to prevent confession from becoming odious, was applicable to all.—St. Alphonsus Liguori, *Theologia Moralis* (ed. L. Gaudé, 4 vols., Romae, 1905-1912), lib. VI, n. 656.

[80] S.C.S. Off., decr. 18 nov. 1682—*Fontes,* n. 758; St. Alphonsus, *Theologia Moralis,* lib. VI, n. 657.

[81] Cf. canons 890, 891; Piatus, *Praelectiones Juris Regularis,* I, 51, 121.

[82] S. Raymundus de Pennafort, *Summa* (ed. nova, Veronae, 1744), lib. I, tit. VIII, cap. 10.

[83] *Summa,* lib. III, tit. XXXIV, cap. 4.

expressly restricted him from hearing the confessions of novices.[84] However, there arose a considerable discussion over the validity of the confessions of novices made to secular priests with faculties only from the ordinary of the place.[85] The discussion centered about the question of jurisdiction and exemption. Suffice it to point out here that the regulations concerning the confessions of the novices were not strict precepts, but rather merely indicated what was to be the general practice. Therefore just as the law did not grant the local Superior the faculty to delegate another to hear the confessions of novices, neither did it on the other hand declare invalid the confessions of novices made to priests approved by the local ordinary to hear the confessions only of seculars.[86] The stricter opinion, based on the notion of the privilege of exemption, and of the consequent necessity of jurisdiction from the regular Superior, maintained that such confessions were invalid, unless it was the intention of the regular Superior to permit them.[87]

Suarez (1548-1617) and Lehmkuhl (1834-1918) held that this latter opinion was the more probable one. However, their contention does not seem to have been supported by the Sacred Congregation of Religious. For in 1914 the Congregation declared that novices of any religious Order, Congregation or Institute whatsoever participated in the privilege already clearly enjoyed by professed members of such communities,[88] namely, of confessing to any priest approved by the ordinary of the place, and of being validly and licitly absolved,

[84] Ojetti, *Synopsis*, "Novitius"; Ferraris, *Prompta Bibliotheca, Canonica, Iuridica, Moralis, Theologica, necnon Ascetica, Polemica, Rubricistica, Historica* (8 vols., Romae, 1757-1762), "Novitius," nn. 14, 15, and "Approbatio," art. II, n. 2. (Hereafter this work will be cited as *Prompta Bibliotheca*).

[85] Ferraris, *Prompta Bibliotheca*, "Approbatio," art. II, nn. 3-5; Suarez, *De Religione*, tract. VII, lib. II, cap. 17, n. 16; Lehmkuhl, *Theologia Moralis*, II, 287; Marc, *Institutiones Morales Alphonsianae* (9. ed., 2 vols., Romae, 1898), II, n. 1762.

[86] Ojetti, *Synopsis*, "Novitius"; Ferraris, *Prompta Bibliotheca*, "Approbatio," art. II, nn. 3-5.

[87] Suarez, *De Religione*, tract. VII, lib. II, cap. 17, n. 16; Lehmkuhl, *Theologia Moralis*, II, 287.

[88] S.C. de Religiosis, decr. 5 aug. 1913—*Fontes*, n. 4418.

even from censures reserved in the Order or Institute, without the need of having the confessor ask permission from the religious Superior.[89]

Obviously the question of novices confessing to the Novice Master did not arise in the case of lay religious Institutes. Attention is called here, however, to the law of the Council of Trent, which obliged Bishops and other Superiors of the monasteries of nuns to provide an extraordinary confessor for the nuns two or three times a year.[90] Since this was a favorable law, it applied also to the novices; but, since the reason for the law was the safeguarding of the liberty of conscience, there was no obligation resting on the novices actually to confess to the extraordinary confessor. It was sufficient for them merely to present themselves to him and to ask his blessing. The novices were free to confess to such a confessor, but there was no obligation to do so.[91]

B. Commentary on the Present Law

The present law of the Code forbids the Novice Master and his *Socius* to hear the confessions of the novices under their care, unless the novices themselves for a grave and urgent reason freely ask it of them in particular cases.[92] This law departs from the old monastic practice, eventually incorporated into the law itself, which reserved to the Novice Master alone the duty of hearing the novices' confessions. This departure was made, according to Larraona,[93] at the express decision of Pope Pius X that both the liberty of conscience and the sanctity of the Sacrament of Penance might above all things be safeguarded. In place of the older custom and law, the Code follows rather the decree of the Holy Office of 1899.[94]

89 S.C. de Religiosis, *Romana et aliarum*, 3 maii 1914—*Fontes*, n. 4421. This legislation was the immediate juridical antecedent of canons 519 and 522.

90 Sess. XXV, *de regularibus*, c. 10.

91 Piatus, *Praelectiones Juris Regularis*, I, 436, 437.

92 Canon 891: Magister novitiorum eiusque socius, . . . sacramentales confessiones suorum alumnorum secum in eadem domo commorantium ne audiant, nisi alumni ex gravi et urgenti causa in casibus particularibus sponte id petant.

93 "Commentarium Codicis"—*CpRM*, XXV (1946), 10-11.

94 S.C.S. Off., 5 iul. 1899—*Fontes*, n. 1225.

According to Wernz-Vidal[95] the prohibition of canon 891 is no stricter than that of canon 518, § 2, which forbids religious Superiors to hear the confessions of their subjects unless a subject freely and spontaneously asks it. The reason assigned for this is that in the case of a novice it can more easily happen that there will be reason for seeking spiritual direction of the Novice Master in a determined case, or of asking advice to conquer a temptation, which certainly is a grave cause.

Several authors, on the other hand, state that the prohibition concerning the Novice Master and his *Socius* is stricter than that established for religious Superiors.[96] None of the authors cited offer any extensive arguments to support their contention. Apparently they are satisfied that a comparison of the wording of the two canons is sufficient evidence. Indeed, such a comparison does seem to demonstrate the point sufficiently. For, as regards the Superiors, the law allows them to hear the confessions of those subjects who freely and spontaneously ask it of them. Only in cases wherein the Superior is the habitual confessor of a subject is a grave reason required.[97] On the other hand, the law expressly prohibits the Novice Master and his *Socius* without a grave and urgent reason to hear the confessions of the novices subject to them, and then only in particular cases and provided that the novice concerned freely asks it of them.[98]

The phrase "in particular cases" offers some difficulty. Many authors interpret it to mean that the Master and his *Socius* are altogether forbidden to be the ordinary and habitual confessors of the novices under their care.[99] This particular case, however, as

[95] *Ius Canonicum,* III, n. 287.

[96] Schaefer, *De Religiosis,* p. 543; Coronata, *Institutiones,* I, n. 586, note 10; Creusen-Garesché-Ellis, *Religious Men and Women in the Code,* p. 163; Chelodi-Ciprotti, *Ius Canonicum de Personis,* p. 424, note 2; Goyeneche, "Consultatio"—*CpR,* XIV (1933), 260; Berutti, "De Confessariis Religiosorum"—*Jus Pontificium* (Romae, 1921—), XIII (1933), 85. (Hereafter this periodical will be cited as *JP*).

[97] Canon 518, § 2.

[98] Canon 891.

[99] Schaefer, *De Religiosis,* p. 543; Raus, *Institutiones Canonicae,* p. 410; Vermeersch-Creusen, *Epitome,* II, n. 170; Creusen-Garesché-Ellis, *Religious Men and Women in the Code,* p. 163; Larraona, "Commentarium Codicis"—*CpRM,* XXV (1946), 14.

Vermeesch-Creusen remark, does not necessarily mean one individual case or instance, but rather a case in which there is some special reason. This special reason, in turn, could be present over a series, even a prolonged series, of individual instances.

Papi expressed the opinion that the Novice Master cannot lawfully be the ordinary confessor of any novice subject to him.[100] This, he rightly maintained seemed to be the better interpretation and more in keeping with the context of the law. However, he admitted that the interpretation which contended that the law allowed the Novice Master to be the ordinary confessor to this or that novice, provided that he was not the ordinary confessor for the whole group of novices, was a probable opinion, and hence could be followed until the Holy See should give an authentic interpretation rendering it untenable.

The law further requires that a grave and urgent reason be present. According to Cappello[101] and Iorio[102] this condition is fulfilled if a novice seriously and spontaneously asks the Novice Master or his *Socius* to hear his confession for the peace of his conscience. Such a request might be made because of some anxiety of conscience that is troubling him, or because he cannot approach another confessor to whom he can manifest his anxiety, especially if the time for Holy Communion is at hand. It could also be requested out of a desire to receive greater or better spiritual direction concerning some anxiety of conscience.

Fanfani is of the opinion that this condition is verified not only when a serious sin has been committed, but also when the novice wishes to dispose himself better for Holy Communion, if he thinks that he is not properly disposed, and also when he has the desire for special counsel or advice.[103] Other authors explain this condition in similar ways.[104]

[100] *Religious In Church Law,* pp. 64-65.

[101] *De Sacramentis,* II, pars. I, n. 422.

[102] *Theologia Moralis* (6. ed., 3 vols., Neapoli: D'Auria, 1938-1939), III, n. 533, 3°.

[103] *De Iure Religiosorum,* n. 213.

[104] Cf. Berutti, *De Religiosis,* pp. 182-183; Vermeersch-Creusen, *Epitome,* II, n. 170; McCormick, *Confessors of Religious,* p. 51; Gerster a Zeil, *Ius Religiosorum* (Taurini: Marietti, 1935), p. 99.

Though the prohibition of canon 891 is of itself a grave one,[105] it is quite generally held by commentators that it does not affect the validity of confessions made against its prescriptions.[106] But such confessions as are made in disregard of the conditions of canon 891 are unlawful, but only on the part of the minister.[107] Still, even though the canon does not affect the validity of the confession, it does not on the other hand automatically confer on the Novice Master and his *Socius* the necessary jurisdiction to hear the confessions of the novices.[108] Rather, the canon supposes that jurisdiction has already been obtained either from the local ordinary or, in the case of exempt clerical religious, from the competent major Superior.[109] The use of this jurisdiction is in turn prohibited except under the conditions established by the law itself.

Where more than one *Socius* has been assigned to assist the Master, each of these is bound by the prescriptions of canon 891.[110] The prohibition however is made only in regard to novices in the strict sense. Yet it contemplates both choir and lay novices. Hence neither postulants nor the newly professed who may still be subject to the Novice Master come under this prohibition.[111] Moreover, the prohibition affects the novices for the whole time during which they are subject to the Novice Master, even should this be for two years or more. But it would not affect those novices who are in their second year of novitiate should they then be assigned to a house other than the novitiate house, since then they would not be subject to the Novice Master during that period.[112]

105 Cappello, *De Sacramentis,* II, pars. I, n. 422.

106 Cf. Schaefer, *De Religiosis,* p. 543; Vermeersch-Creusen, *Epitome,* II, n. 170; Wernz-Vidal, *Ius Canonicum,* III, n. 287; Coronata, *Institutiones,* I, n. 586, note 10; Cappello, *De Sacramentis,* II, pars. I, n. 422.

107 Iorio, *Theologia Moralis,* III, n. 533, 1°.

108 Vermeersch-Creusen, *Epitome,* II, n. 170; Cappello, *De Sacramentis,* II, pars. I, n. 422; Ciprotti, "Adhuc de seminarii rectore an ordinariam iurisdictionem habeat ad alumnorum confessiones audiendas"—*Apollinaris,* VIII (1935), 609-610.

109 Cf. canons 874, § 1; 875, § 1.

110 Larraona, "Commentarium Codicis"—*CpRM,* XXV (1946), 11.

111 Fanfani, *De Iure Religiosorum,* n. 214; Vito, *De Religiosis,* p. 212; Larraona, "Commentarium Codicis"—*CpRM,* XXV (1946), 13.

112 Larraona, "Commentarium Codicis"—*CpRM,* XXV (1946), 13.

The Novice Master is forbidden to hear the confessions of only those novices who are subject to him. Hence, should there be two Novice Masters in the one novitiate house, one in charge of the choir novices, the other in charge of the lay novices, each Master would be allowed to hear the confessions of those novices who belong to the group not subject to himself.[113]

It is clear from the dispositions of the law that the spiritual direction of the novices, even in clerical exempt religious Institutes, is divided between the Novice Master and the confessor. Yet the chief part of this direction is the province of the Master, a fact which the confessor will do well to remember.[114] In lay religious Institutes, however, the more intimate matters of one's spiritual life ought rather to be reserved for the confessor. None the less, even in these Institutes the Novice Master, because of his qualities and the confidence he inspires in the novices, is or should be a competent guide and counselor in these matters. It can be said that it is the Novice Master's office to direct the novices in regard to the religious life as led in the community concerned, while it belongs to the confessor to direct them in the religious life as such.[115]

Besides the ordinary confessor, or confessors, for the novices[116] there are to be designated other confessors whom the novices can freely approach in particular cases to go to confession. In such cases the Master is strictly forbidden to show any displeasure at the novices approaching these confessors.[117] From the wording of the law it seems that at least two such confessors are to be appointed. The Novice Master must remember that he is forbidden to impede the novices, either directly or indirectly, from enjoying the concession of the law which allows them to approach these confessors. Still the discipline of the novitiate must be observed. Therefore, ordinarily the novices should not go out of the novitiate to approach one of the

[113] Larraona, *art. cit., loc. cit.*

[114] Wernz-Vidal, *Ius Canonicum,* III, n. 287; Schaefer, *De Religiosis,* p. 543; Creusen-Garesché-Ellis, *Religious Men and Women in the Code,* p. 163.

[115] Vermeersch-Creusen, *Epitome,* I, n. 665.

[116] Cf. canon 566, § 2, 1°, 2°.

[117] Canon 566, § 2, 3°.

supplementary confessors.[118] If this is necessary, permission of the Novice Master is in order. Likewise his permission is required for the novice to absent himself from some exercise or duty in which he should be engaged at the time he wishes to go to confession. Similarly if the confessor has to be summoned from outside, this would ordinarily have to be done through the agency of the Novice Master.[119]

The Novice Master cannot rightfully forbid the novices in any way whatsoever to confess to priests other than those designated as confessors to the novices. Nor can he tell them that they cannot lawfully approach the extraordinary confessor more than four times a year, or more than once in three months. Such statements would manifestly be contrary to the law, and hence untrue.[120]

Nowhere does the law speak of the frequency with which the novices are to go to confession. The Clementine Constitution on the other hand required that novices confess at least twice a month.[121] The Code requires that religious confess at least once a week.[122] Interpreting this law in the light of the purpose of the novitiate [123] and in the light of the Constitution *Cum ad regularem,* one may well consider it applicable also to the novices. Hence, it appears legitimate for the Novice Master in his private talks with the novices to inquire whether they go to confession regularly. However, he may not ask to whom the novice goes to confession, much less if he ever goes to a confessor other than one designated as a confessor to the novices.[124]

Similarly, a Novice Mistress who would inquire into the reason why a novice wishes to confess to one of the supplementary or to one

[118] Berutti, "De Confessariis Religiosorum"—*JP,* XIII (1933), 86-87.

[119] Kinane, "The Confessors of Novices in Religious Institutes of Men"—*The Irish Ecclesiastical Record* (Dublin, 1864—), 5. series, XLI (1933), 88. (Hereafter this periodical will be cited as *IER.*)

[120] Cf. canons 519; 522; 523; 566, § 2, 4°.

[121] Clemens VIII, const. *"Cum ad regularem,"* 19 mart. 1603, § 9—*Fontes,* n. 189.

[122] Canon 595, § 1, 3°.

[123] Cf. canon 565, § 1.

[124] Cf. canons 566; 519.

of the occasional confessors,[125] or who would show herself displeased at this, would certainly offend against the spirit of the law. Still, for such conduct she would not be subject to the penalties threatened by canon 2414. For this canon speaks only of Superioresses. Hence, since penal laws are to be interpreted strictly,[126] Novice Mistresses are not to be considered as included under the classification of Superioresses as mentioned in this canon.

[125] Cf. canons 521, § 3; 522; 523.
[126] Canon 19.

CHAPTER VI

INSTRUCTION OF THE NOVICES

Article 1. Spiritual Training

The essence of the novitiate lies in the mutual probation which both the religious Institute and the candidate undergo.[1] The Council of Trent had demanded for the validity of the profession that this probation last for a full year.[2] It was to insure still further the adequacy of the probationary period that Clement VIII issued his Constitution *Cum ad regularem*. Still, the exact nature of the probation was left by the law to the customs and requirements of the various religious Institutes and to the Master of Novices.

The law, however, did give a general outline of how the Novice Master was to train and prove the novices. It required that he be diligent in exercising the novices in the regular observance, giving them an appreciation for the excellence of their vocation and the meaning of the vows. Likewise the Master was to instruct them in mental and vocal prayer, in the custody of the senses, in mortification and in the other customary ascetical practices.[3] Inasmuch as these norms embraced the essential elements of knowledge required for the validity of a religious profession, they limited the possibility of a plea of nullity of profession on the basis of ignorance.[4]

[1] Wernz, *Ius Decretalium*, III, tit. XXIV, n. 633.

[2] "In quacumque religione tam virorum quam mulierum professio non fiat ante decimum sextum annum expletum, nec qui minore tempore quam per annum post susceptum habitum in probatione steterit, ad professionem admittatur. Professio autem antea facta sit nulla. . . ."—Sess. XXV, *de regularibus*, c. 15.

[3] Clemens VIII, const. "*Cum ad regularem*," 19 mart. 1603, § 9—*Fontes*, n. 189.

[4] "Irrita autem est Professio, facta ab eo, qui ignorabat Regulam, saltem circa substantialia. . . . Non quaelibet autem ignorantia et error removet consensum et irritat obligationem. Necesse enim est, ut ignorantia sit invincibilis, scilicet ea, quae manet post adhibitam diligentiam. Quare cum Novitius facile potuerit erudiri in novitiatu de iis, quae ad vota pertinebant, sive a Magistro

These were general norms applicable both to those preparing for the priesthood and to those aspiring to the lay brotherhood. However, with regard to the latter the Constitution *Cum ad regularem* established some special regulations. The lay novices were to have their own quarters, as far as it was possible, separate from the quarters used by the prospective clerics. Moreover they were to be diligently instructed in spiritual matters, especially in mental prayer, according to their capacity. Finally, they were obliged to attend the spiritual conferences given by the Novice Master.[5] In 1911 the Holy See required that the doctrinal instructions given to novices aspiring to the lay brotherhood in religious Orders be given according to the Catechism of the Council of Trent. These novices were likewise to receive special conferences embracing not only the catechism but also the principles of the spiritual life, the explanations of the rule and constitutions, particularly the rules pertaining to the lay religious, and likewise instructions in the canons of Christian politeness and manners.[6]

The present law similarly charges the Novice Master with the grave obligation of employing all diligence in assiduously training the novices in religious discipline in accordance with the constitutions of the Institute and with the norms of canon 565.[7] This grave and important obligation is a personal one imposed on the Master, and not on the *Socius*.[8] Evidently, then, he is bound to consecrate all his efforts and use every legitimate means to give the novices a complete and well-rounded formation in the religious life and discipline.

Novitiorum, sive a Sociis in tyrocinio; et tamen omisit hanc notitiam acquirere, eius ignorantia est prorsus vincibilis, et aequiparatur scientiae."—S. C. C., *Nullitas Professionis*, 18 sept. 1802—Pallottini, *Collectio Omnium Conclusionum et Resolutionum Quae in Causis Propositis apud Sacram Congregationem Cardinalium S. Concilii Tridentini Interpretum Prodierunt ab eius Institutione Anno MCLXIV ad MDCCCLX, Distinctis Titulis Alphabetico Ordine per Materias Digesta* (18 vols., Romae, 1868-1895), XV, 434.

[5] Clemens VIII, const. *"Cum ad regularem,"* 19 mart. 1603, § 15—*Fontes*, n. 189.

[6] S.C. de Religiosis, decr., 1 ian. 1911—*Fontes*, n. 4407.

[7] Canon 562.

[8] Blat, *Ius de Religiosis*, 345; Larraona, "Commentarium Codicis"—*CpRM*, XXIV (1943), 117.

The gravity of this obligation is seen from the fact that not only the personal perfection of the members, but also the whole religious spirit of the province and even of the Institute itself depend in large measure upon that adequate training and solid formation which it is the purpose of the novitiate to give.[9]

It is because of the importance of this task that the Novice Master is to be free of all duties and offices that could hinder him in the care of the novices. Similarly, if it is necessary, he is to be assisted by a *Socius* in the government of the novitiate, so that the Novice Master may devote himself entirely to the paramount duty of training and forming the novices in the religious life.[10]

The novices are to be trained according to the spirit of the Institute and in accord with its rule and constitutions. Hence the Novice Master is not at liberty to imbue them with ideas of spirituality and religious discipline, his own or otherwise, which are not consonant with the rule and constitutions of the Institute concerned, even should these ideas be perfectly laudable in themselves.[11]

Novice Masters would do well to remember the admonition of Pius XI in which he exhorted all religious to remain faithful to the example and teaching of their respective founders. If they wish to partake fully of the graces of their vocation, so wrote the Pope, let them follow the example set them by their founder, and preserve his honor by obeying his admonitions and imbibing his spirit.[12]

[9] Cf. Larraona, "Commentarium Codicis"—*CpRM*, XXIV (1943), 117; Pius XI, ep. apost. *"Unigenitus Dei Filius,"* 19 mart. 1924: "Neque tirones unquam obliviscantur, quales in novitiatu fuerint, tales se in reliquum vitae tempus futuros, et supplendi posterius renovato animo tirocinii, si semel modico aut nullo fructu illud egerint, spem esse plerumque inanissimam."—*AAS*, XVI (1924), 142.

[10] Canon 559, §§ 2, 3; cf. Larraona, "Commentarium Codicis"—*CpRM*, XXIV (1943), 117-118.

[11] Larraona, "Commentarium Codicis"—*CpRM*, XXIV (1943), 118.

[12] Pius XI, ep. apost. *"Unigenitus Dei Filius,"* 19 mart. 1924: "Ac primum omnium religiosos viros cohortamur, ut suum quisque Conditorem Patremque legiferum in exemplum intueantur, si velint gratiarum, quae a sua ipsorum vocatione proficiscuntur, certo esse copioseque participes. . . . Quare eo sodales, optimorum instar filiorum, curas cogitationesque convertant, ut Patris legiferi

To assist the novices in acquiring a true religious spirit the Master can and should demand that they have personal interviews with him. The purpose of these interviews is to afford the Master an opportunity not only to correct defects which he may have noticed, but also to instruct each novice according to his personal needs and capacity. For although general instructions and conferences must be given in common to all the novices, it remains true that each individual differs in temperament and character. Therefore a degree of personal direction is required. In these interviews, however, the Master, particularly in lay religious Institutes, must be cautious not to transgress into the sphere reserved for the confessor.[13]

The scope or purpose of the year of novitiate is outlined in canon 565. Under the discipline of the Master, the novices are to devote themselves to the study of the rules and constitutions and to assiduous prayer and meditation. Moreover they are to be engaged in learning well everything pertaining to the vows and virtues, and in following those opportune exercises of the novitiate which are calculated to aid them in extirpating the seeds of vice, in governing their passions and in acquiring virtue.[14]

The study of the rule and constitutions is absolutely necessary to the novices, since logically they must first know the nature of the obligations which these impose before they can oblige themselves by vow to the observance of them. Hence, the *Normae* of 1901 required that from the very beginning of the year of probation each novice was to be given a complete copy of the constitutions of the Institute.[15] According to Larraona this same obligation is always expressly inserted in the constitutions of the more recent Institutes.[16] Similarly, one of the questions (n. 18) which must be answered in the quinquennial report to be made by the Superiors General and the Mothers

honorem tueantur, eius cum et praescriptis et monitis obsequendo, tum imbibendo spiritum; neque enim e statu suo decident usque dum Conditoris sui vestigiis institerint."—*AAS*, XVI (1924), 135.

[13] Cf. Larraona, "Commentarium Codicis"—*CpRM,* XXIV (1943), 118-119.

[14] Canon 565, § 1.

[15] Art. 87, 321.

[16] "Commentarium Codicis"—*CpRM,* XXIV (1943), 211.

General of Congregations of simple vows is concerned with the matter of whether or not the novices have a complete copy of the constitutions.[17]

Some canonists are of the opinion that it is sufficient if each novice has a summary or a compendium of the constitutions, provided that he can always consult the complete text in the library of the novitiate.[18] On the other hand, Schaefer[19] maintains that according to the intention of the Holy See a compendium is not sufficient, and that the novices must have a complete copy of the constitutions from the beginning of the novitiate. Beste and Bastien are of the same opinion.[20]

It appears however that some distinctions are in order. In those more recently approved Institutes whose constitutions require that a complete copy of the constitutions be given to the novices from the very beginning of the novitiate, a summary would evidently be insufficient. In the older Institutes where no such obligation exists, the customary practice of giving the novices only a summary of the constitutions appears to be legitimate. This would be the case especially if such a compendium had been drawn up for the special use of the novices and approved as such by the Superior General. Such a summary would, or should contain the basic and more important rules and obligations of the Institute concerned. Yet it would still seem required that there be a complete copy always easily available to the novices. Moreover, the complete copy of the constitutions should be given to the novices at least by the time the Master begins explaining in his conferences the *details* of the obligations imposed by the vows, the rules and the constitutions.

The Novice Master must likewise instruct the novices on the importance and the method of prayer and meditation. Moreover, he must see to it that they practice what they learn, and thus show

[17] The Latin text of the formulary to be answered in the quinquennial report is found in *AAS,* XIV (1922), 278-286, the official English translation in *AAS,* XV (1923), 459-466.

[18] Creusen-Garesché-Ellis, *Religious Men and Women in the Code,* p. 157.

[19] *De Religiosis,* p. 536.

[20] Beste, *Introductio in Codicem,* p. 376; Bastien, *Directoire Canonique,* p. 327, n. 462 and note 3.

signs of acquiring a spirit of prayer. Similarly he is to exercise them in the practice of mortification as an essential counterpart of prayer in eradicating the seeds of vice and in acquiring virtue.[21] In all these matters the customary ascetical practices of each Institute will have to be the norm for carrying out in detail the general prescriptions of the common law.

In connection with his instructions on the vow of poverty, the Novice Master should acquaint the novices of their obligation to appoint an administrator of any property they may possess. It will be his duty to administer this property during the time they will be bound by simple vows. Similarly, novices in religious Congregations must make a will *mortis causa,* in which will they dispose of any goods they possess or will possess in the future.[22]

The law makes a special provision that the lay novices in Institutes both of men and of women religious be diligently instructed in Christian doctrine. For this purpose a special conference must be given them at least once a week.[23] Since the Code uses the word "*praeterea,*" these instructions must be given over and above the instructions on the religious life and the regular observance as given to all the novices in common. They must be special instructions in the sense that they must be accommodated to the mental capacity of the novices. If this is fulfilled, there seems to be no reason in law why others, the professed lay religious for instance, could not also attend these instructions.[24] Berutti remarks [25] that the instructions should last about one hour, unless the number and mental capacity of the novices warrant a shorter period. Likewise, it does not seem contrary to the law to suspend these instructions during the hot summer months. For a just cause these instructions could be given by another competent religious besides the Novice Master. In lay

[21] Larraona, "Commentarium Codicis"—*CpRM,* XXIV (1943), 211-212.

[22] Canons 569, §§ 1, 3; cf. canons 580, 581.

[23] Canon 565, § 2. This is stricter than the law concerning professed lay religious. For the latter two catechetical instructions a month suffice.—Canon 509, § 2, 2°.

[24] Larraona, "Commentarium Codicis"—*CpRM, XXIV* (1943), 213.

[25] *De Religiosis,* p. 178.

religious Institutes of women the chaplain or confessor might well fulfill this duty.

In speaking of this obligation the Code uses the word *"conversi."* This word is not strictly synonymous with "lay religious." Rather, it refers to those who are engaged in the manual and domestic services of the community whether this latter be lay or clerical.[26] Hence, it appears from the general law itself that in lay institutes this special catechetical instruction needs to be given only to those who are engaged in the manual or domestic services of the community. It need not be given to those novices who are destined to be teachers or nurses, for example.

With a view to the general law alone, this seems a valid conclusion. But the instruction of the Sacred Congregation of Religious, issued on November 25, 1929, must also be considered. This instruction was addressed to the Superiors and Superioresses General of lay religious families. It requires that all postulants and novices in these Institutes be given courses of instruction in religion. The document further demands of postulants and novices that they know and be able to explain the Christian doctrine satisfactorily. None may be admitted to profession until they have acquired this knowledge and have successfully passed an examination thereon.[27]

This requirement of the instruction clearly seems to apply to *all* postulants and novices in these Institutes, whether they be choir or lay novices.[28] It is not to be confused with the second requisite of the instruction which requires that *after* the novitiate is over those religious who are destined to be engaged in teaching catechism be duly trained in catechism and in the methods of teaching it to others, and are further to be examined in both these points by the ordinary or his delegate.[29]

These special catechetical instructions therefore must be given

[26] Vermeersch-Creusen, *Epitome,* I, n. 616; Schaefer, *De Religiosis,* p. 453.

[27] S.C. de Religiosis, instr. 25 nov. 1929, n. 1—*AAS,* XXII (1930), 29.

[28] Cf. Creusen-Garesché-Ellis, *Religious Men and Women in the Code,* p. 157.

[29] S.C. de Religiosis, instr. 25 nov. 1929, n. 2—*AAS,* XXII (1930), 29; cf. Schaefer, *De Religiosis,* p. 321.

to the lay novices in all clerical Orders and Congregations in virtue of the prescription of canon 565, § 2. They must likewise be given to all postulants and novices in all lay Institutes, both of men and of women, if not by reason of the general law, then at least by reason of the instruction of the Sacred Congregation of Religious. This is logical, for an accurate and serious instruction in Christian doctrine is especially necessary at the present time when so many grave errors about God, religion, the rational soul, human society, and man's eternal destiny, are rampant everywhere. A knowledge of the truths of our holy faith furthermore nourishes and fortifies the faith itself. Hence it is particularly necessary for those who intend to dedicate themselves to the service of God in the religious state.[30] The further instructions on the methods of teaching catechism to others need be given only to those who are destined to teach catechism, and then only after the completion of the novitiate.

Novice Masters and Mistresses would do well to remember that in instructing the novices they must not bring any undue force or duress whatsoever to bear upon the novices in order to influence them in making their profession of vows. A profession of vows made under force, grave fear or deceit is invalid.[31] Furthermore, the law inflicts the non-reserved but automatic penalty (*ipso facto*) of excommunication upon anyone, regardless of dignity, who should in any way whatsoever force a novice to make the profession of vows.[32] A Novice Master or Mistress, of course, would have to be gravely culpable in bringing such force (grave fear is sufficient) to bear on the novice, and the crime would have to be perfect in its kind as defined by the law.[33] But should that be the case, the Novice Master or Mistress would by that fact be excommunicated.[34]

During the year of the novitiate the novices are not to be engaged in hearing confessions, in delivering sermons, or in the external works

[30] Cf. S.C. de Religiosis, instr. 25 nov. 1929—*AAS*, XXII (1930), 28-29.

[31] Canon 572, § 1, 4°.

[32] Canon 2352.

[33] Cf. canons 2218, § 2; 2228.

[34] Concerning the influence of grave fear on the validity of profession cf. Oesterle, "De relationibus inter metum gravem et invaliditatem novitiatus et professionis"—*CpR*, XV (1934), 386-411.

of the institute.[35] The Code here is treating of the canonical year of the novitiate, which alone is prescribed by law, and which alone is necessary for a valid profession, unless a contrary provision be expressly made by particular law.[36] Yet, it is clear from the instruction of the Sacred Congregation of Religious that it is the wish of the Holy See that the second year of the novitiate, if such is required, be conducted in general as is the first year.[37] The question of the second year of the novitiate will be considered more at length in the following chapter.

The law demands that the novices be free of these duties so that nothing, not even the work of the priestly ministry, may interfere with their training and probation. No distinction is made by the law, and hence a novice who is already a priest is forbidden to hear confessions or deliver sermons even within the novitiate itself. It seems, however, that it is the habitual occupation with these matters that is forbidden, since the law uses the phrase *ne destinentur novitii*, that is, the novices shall not be destined for these works. Therefore, if a novice were occasionally asked to preach or to hear confessions, this seems to be allowed by the Code. Such a case might arise if occasionally such a novice's assistance were needed in the confessional because of the great number of people waiting to go to confession. It might likewise be permitted on occasion as a means of trying the novice's virtue. For example, he might be told to prepare a sermon, or to hear confessions, at a time when the rest of the novices are engaged in recreation.[38] It is clear, however, that a novice who is a priest would be not only permitted, but, *servandis servatis*, even obliged to hear the confession of a person in danger of death.[39]

The lay novices, however, are permitted to be engaged within the novitiate house itself in the duties of the lay brothers. Still they are not to be the primary officials in charge of these duties, nor are the duties to interfere with the exercises of the novitiate which

[35] Canon 565, § 3.

[36] Canon 555, § 2.

[37] S.C. de Religiosis, instr. 3 nov. 1921—*AAS*, XIII (1921), 539-540.

[38] Wernz-Vidal, *Ius Canonicum*, III, n. 286; cf. Larraona, "Commentarium Codicis"—*CpRM*, XXIV (1943), 214.

[39] Canon 882.

these novices must attend.[40] Should a lay novice be the only one engaged in some particular task, then it appears, as Larraona remarks, that he could not be called a "primary official" in the strict sense,[41] which implies that he has others subordinate to himself. This could well be the case with the minor tasks of the house. Moreover, the novice would ultimately be responsible to the Novice Master and under his guidance. The Master in turn should so direct the novice that the duties in which he is engaged do not interfere with the exercises of the novitiate. For this same reason it seems permissible to allow a lay novice who is expert or skilled in some particular art or craft to be the technical director or advisor of other novices or even of professed lay brothers who lack the skill.[42]

Article 2. Studies in the Novitiate

In the legislation of Clement VIII no mention was made of studies in the novitiate. Indeed, the whole tenor of the Constitution *Cum ad regularem* indicated that the year of the novitiate was to be given exclusively to spiritual exercises. It implied rather that studies were to be undertaken only after the profession.[43] The Holy See, of course, never wished anything to interfere with the essentially spiritual character of the novitiate training. Indeed, the Sacred Congregation of Bishops and Regulars refused to approve a proposed scheme of novitiate that was part novitiate and part scholasticate.[44] The *Normae* of 1901 expressly forbade studies in the novitiate. At most they permitted a moderate degree of study under the careful surveillance of the Novice Master during the second year of the novitiate.[45]

In 1910 the Holy See altered its attitude toward the question of studies in the novitiate. It prescribed a certain amount of study during the year of probation.[46] This was to consist of one hour's

[40] Canon 565, § 3.

[41] "Commentarium Codicis"—*CpRM*, XXIV (1943), 216.

[42] Larraona, *art. cit.*, p. 216.

[43] Cf. Clemens VIII, const. *"Cum ad regularem,"* 19 mart. 1603, § 20—*Fontes*, n. 189; Schaefer, *De Religiosis*, p. 539.

[44] *AJP*, V (1861), 181.

[45] *Normae*, art. 73, 74.

[46] S.C. de Religiosis, decr. 27 aug. 1910—*Fontes*, n. 4405.

private study a day, except on feast days, and three classes a week of an hour each under the guidance of the Novice Master, his *Socius*, or an extern professor. The decree expressly declared that it was not the intention of the legislator to make a school of the novitiate; yet, on the other hand, the studies were not to become a mere exercise of mortification for the novices. The type of study was to correspond to the nature of the Order or the Congregation concerned. The Novice Master was to be the moderator of the studies, and was to form a judgment of the talents and of the sedulous application to study on the part of each novice.

Though the nature of the studies was to be determined by the Superiors, still it was prescribed that the novices were to study their native language, and that those who were destined for the priesthood were to study Latin and Greek as well, or at least repeat what they had already learned in their previous schooling in these subjects. The writings of the Fathers of the Church and of the ancient ecclesiastical writers were especially commended. It was suggested, too, that the novices who aspired to the clerical state occasionally speak Latin, develop their memories, and acquire a certain fluency for speaking in public.[47]

This decree as such was not restricted to those who aspired to the clerical state. Still it seems that it was restricted to those who by virtue of their future profession would be engaged in intellectual pursuits. Hence it was not obligatory on lay novices destined to do domestic work, nor on religious Institutes given to the corporal works of mercy. And since it was a *moderate* amount of study that was prescribed, the Superiors and especially the Novice Master had to exercise care and vigilance, lest the study be carried to excess to the detriment of the spiritual character of the novitiate training. Finally, though daily study was required, it seemed equitable if some days, holidays for example, days of special spiritual exercises and retreat, which could not be dovetailed very well with study, were excepted.[48]

Regarding the present force of this decree it is the common

[47] S.C. de Religiosis, decr. 27 aug. 1910, nn. 1-3—*Fontes,* n. 4405.

[48] Cf. Vermeersch, "De aliqua in noviciatu studiis opera danda"—*Periodica,* V (1913), 196-197.

opinion of canonists that, since it is contrary to the present law of the Code, it is no longer binding.[49] The present law forbids the novices to pursue the formal study of letters, of the sciences, or of the arts during the year of the novitiate.[50]

By using the words *dedita opera* the Code seems to forbid all *formal* study. In other words, since the novitiate is essentially the proving ground where the fitness of the novices for the religious life is tested, study must not be made the principal work. This would only distract the novices from the principal work, their spiritual formation.[51]

Still it is to be noted that the decree of 1910 is cited in the footnotes of the Code as the only source of canon 565, § 3. Moreover, although the law forbids formal study, it does not necessarily follow that all study is prohibited. Hence many authors interpret the law to mean that some moderate study is permissible during the year of the novitiate.[52] But the object of this study should not be the acquisition of new knowledge, but rather the retention and review of knowledge already acquired. Accordingly, the subject matter should be in keeping with the character and nature of each Institute. The Superiors, in turn, will thus have an added opportunity of testing the talents and diligence of the novices.[53]

[49] Canon 6, 1°; cf. Larraona, "Commentarium Codicis"—*CpRM*, XXIV (1943), 215. Nevertheless, as will be seen presently, many authors maintain that the general tenor of this decree may still be observed as a directive norm for allowing a *moderate* amount of study during the novitiate. Cf. Creusen-Garesché-Ellis, *Religious Men and Women in the Code*, p. 158.

[50] Canon 565, § 3: "Anno novitiatus . . . novitii . . . neve dedita opera studiis vacent litterarum, scientiarum aut artium. . . ."

[51] Cf. Pius XI, ep. apost. *"Unigenitus Dei Filius,"* 19 mart. 1924: "Emenso inferiore litterarum curriculo, alumni et candidati omnes, . . . in novitiatum cooptentur, in quo . . . religiosae vitae principia et virtutes data opera perdiscant. . . . Quamobrem, remotis quarumvis disciplinarum studiis atque oblectamentis, huc tantummodo novitii animos intendant, ut sapienti magistri sui ductu, interioris vitae exercitationibus virtutumque adeptioni vacent. . . ."—*AAS*, XVI (1924), 142.

[52] Vermeersch-Creusen, *Epitome*, I, n. 664; Schaefer, *De Religiosis*, p. 541; Wernz-Vidal, *Ius Canonicum*, III, n. 286; Blat, *Ius de Religiosis*, 348; Larraona, "Commentarium Codicis"—*CpRM*, XXIV (1943), 215.

[53] Papi, *Religious In Church Law*, pp. 165-166.

It was never the mind of the Church completely to forbid all study during the novitiate.[54] Hence the decree of 1910 may still be used as a directive norm.[55] It seems permissible therefore to allow and even to require the novices to spend an hour a day in study, and to conduct a lecture two or three times a week. The Novice Master, his *Socius,* or even some other competent religious could take charge of conducting these lectures.[56] But as the novitiate must not become a school room, it seems contrary to the law for the novices to undertake the study of a new language, or of a new science such as philosophy or theology, hitherto unpursued.[57] It does seem lawful, however, to engage the novices in the study of the Gregorian chant and the liturgy, and to refresh their knowledge of an already acquired language by allowing them to read and study the New Testament in that language.

[54] Chelodi-Ciprotti, *Ius Canonicum de Personis,* p. 423, note 2.

[55] Berutti, *De Religiosis,* p. 179; De Meester, *Compendium J. C.,* II, 442, note 1; Beste, *Introductio in Codicem,* p. 377, note 17; Prümmer, *Manuale Iuris Canonici,* p. 281; Raus, *Institutiones Canonicae,* p. 304, note 3.

[56] Cf. S.C. de Religiosis, decr. 27 aug. 1910, nn. 1, 2—*AAS,* II (1910), 730-731.

[57] Cf. Claeys-Bouuaert-Simenon, *Manuale Juris Canonici,* I, 377.

CHAPTER VII

THE SECOND YEAR OF THE NOVITIATE

THE general law requires that the novitiate last for one complete and continuous year.[1] Still it allows of the possibility of a prolongation of the novitiate. This could be either because the novitiate had been interrupted, or because it is dubious whether the novice is sufficiently worthy to be admitted to profession.[2] Likewise the constitutions of a given Institute could require a longer novitiate, usually two years, but in such a case the additional year does not affect the validity of the novitiate, unless it is otherwise expressly stated by the constitutions.[3] Moreover, permission of the Holy See is necessary to transfer the canonical year of the novitiate from the first to the second year. But to dispense with the second year, when this year is not required for a valid novitiate, the permission of the Holy See is necessary only if the Institute is one of pontifical approval. The local ordinary can grant the dispensation when there is question of a diocesan Institute.[4]

The Code considers directly only the canonical year of the novitiate. Yet according to the mind of the Church any prolongation of the novitiate is to be conducted, in general, as is the canonical year.[5] Accordingly the Sacred Congregation of Religious in 1921 issued an instruction on the second year of the novitiate.[6]

This instruction applies only to religious Congregations, not to religious Orders. The reason for this, according to Maroto,[7] is that

[1] Canon 555, § 1, 2°.

[2] Cf. canons 556, § 2; 571, § 2.

[3] Canon 555, § 2.

[4] Cf. The authentic interpretation of canon 555 given by the Pontifical Commission for the authentic interpretation of the Code, Feb. 12, 1935—*AAS*, XXVII (1935), 92; canon 81; Maroto, "Annotationes"—*CpRM*, XVI (1935), 371-376.

[5] Larraona, "Commentarium Codicis"—*CpRM*, XXIV (1943), 213.

[6] S.C. de Religiosis, 3 nov. 1921—*AAS*, XIII (1921), 539-540.

[7] "Annotationes"—*CpR*, III (1922), 40.

only one or the other religious Order has a second year of novitiate, and these were regarded by the Sacred Congregation as already properly ordered and conducted. Furthermore, though instructions issued by the various Sacred Congregations of the Roman Curia usually contain only directive norms, it sometimes happens that they contain obligatory prescriptions. Such is the case with the instruction under consideration. For the Pope commanded it to be observed completely by each and every religious Congregation whose constitutions prescribe a second year of novitiate.[8] Therefore, if the constitutions of an Institute on this matter are at variance with the prescriptions of this instruction, they are to be corrected and brought into accord with them. This is true even if the constitutions have been approved since the promulgation of the Code, but prior to the issuance of the instruction. For the instruction is really a pontifical law issued in such fashion as to derogate from any constitutions contrary to it.[9]

Though canon 565, § 3, speaks directly only of the canonical year of the novitiate, nevertheless its norms apply to the second year as well. This seems clear from the tenor of the Instruction of 1921.[10] For according to this instruction novices may be engaged in the works of the Institute only if the constitutions prescribe it, and provided that the fundamental laws of the novitiate are not transgressed. Therefore, even during the second year of the novitiate, the spiritual formation of the novices must be the chief objective. Hence the Novice Master must continue to exercise them in the regular cbservance and direct them in their efforts to extirpate the seeds of vice and to acquire the virtues requisite for their state in life.[11]

The instruction allows the novices to be engaged in these occupations only in a prudent and moderate manner and solely for the instruction of the novices themselves. They are therefore to be placed under the vigilance and direction of a grave religious who will teach them by word and example. Consequently it is forbidden to

[8] *AAS*, XIII (1921), 539; cf. Maroto, *art. cit.*, pp. 38-39.

[9] Cf. canon 22; Maroto, *art. cit.*, p. 40.

[10] Berutti, *De Religiosis*, p. 179; Maroto, *art. cit.*, p. 41.

[11] S.C. de Religiosis, instr. 3 nov. 1921, n. I—*AAS*, XIII (1921), 539-540.

the Superiors to use the novices primarily for the benefit of the Institute or Community. They may not act as teachers or instructors in schools, whether permanently or only temporarily, during the absence of the usual teachers. Nor can they act as nurses in hospitals.[12]

Even though the constitutions allow the novices during the second year of the novitiate to be engaged in works of the Institute outside the novitiate house, this is to be done only by way of exception and for a grave cause. Such a grave cause would be present if there were not sufficient room in the novitiate house, or if the novices could not properly engage in the occupations of the Institute within the novitiate. But under no pretext whatsoever is necessity or usefulness to the Community a sufficient reason. Accordingly, even though the personnel of professed religious be insufficient for the occupations of the Institute, it is never permitted to use the novices to correct this deficiency.[13]

But in any case, whether the novices be occupied within or outside the novitiate house, they are to cease all these activities two months before profession, and, if outside the novitiate, they must return to it. These two months must then be spent in serious preparation for their profession of vows.[14]

It seems clear from this instruction that the Novice Master, along with the higher Superiors, has a grave obligation of seeing that these rules are observed. For the spiritual training and the religious formation of the novices is the fundamental objective of the novitiate, whether this lasts for one year or longer. Nothing, not even such spiritual and corporal works of mercy as instructing the ignorant and caring for the sick, may supersede or interfere with this basically important formation.

[12] S.C. de Religiosis, instr. 3 nov. 1921, n. II—*AAS*, XIII (1921), 540.

[13] S.C. de Religiosis, instr. 3 nov. 1921, n. III—*AAS*, XIII (1921), 540.

[14] S.C. de Religiosis, instr. 3 nov. 1921, n. IV—*AAS*, XIII (1921), 540. These two months of residence in the novitiate house are not however required for the validity of the profession.—Goyeneche, "Consultatio"—*CpR*, VII (1926), 41.

CONCLUSIONS

As a result of this study the following conclusions are offered:

1. The law of the Code concerning the Novice Master is also applicable to the Novice Mistress in religious Institutes of women, unless the contrary is clear either from the context of the law or from the nature of the matter treated. (p. 18)

2. The general law concerning the Novice Master does not apply to those Societies, whether of men or of women, whose members live in common, but do not profess public vows. (pp. 18-21)

3. The designation of a Novice Master and his habitual residence in the novitiate, though grave obligations, are not required for the validity of the novitiate, or for the validity of the subsequent profession of the novices. (pp. 22-30)

4. The qualifications required of the Novice Master by canon 559, § 1, are required for the lawful appointment of the Novice Master. They are not necessary for the validity of the appointment, much less for the validity of the novitiate and the subsequent profession. (pp. 34-38)

5. In clerical religious Institutes the Novice Master must be a priest even if he is in charge only of lay novices. (pp. 38-39)

6. The *Socius* to the Novice Master has no proper authority by reason of his office. In clerical religious Institutes, the *Socius* need not be a priest. (pp. 44-46)

7. The office of local Superior is not necessarily incompatible with that of the Novice Master. (pp. 50-52)

8. The Novice Master is not a religious Superior in the strict canonical sense. (p. 59)

9. The power of the Novice Master, even in clerical exempt religious Institutes, is neither jurisdictional nor dominative, but rather social or domestic power. (pp. 60-69)

10. The Novice Master is not included among those Superiors who are competent to admit a dying novice to profession. But he may act as the delegate of any of these Superiors. (pp. 86-87)

11. The Novice Master is bound by the letter of the law of canon 530, § 1, and hence is strictly forbidden to demand or urge the novices subject to him to render an account of conscience to him. (pp. 101-106)

12. The Novice Master may never reveal any knowledge gained through sacramental confession or through a manifestation of conscience made to him by a novice. Nor can he use this knowledge in making his report on the novices to the Superiors, or in expressing his opinion concerning a novice's worthiness to be admitted to profession. (pp. 110-113)

13. The Novice Master and his *Socius* are forbidden to be the ordinary confessors for any novices subject to them. If they hear the confession of a novice in disregard of the conditions of canon 891, they act unlawfully, but the confession is valid, provided that they already have the necessary jurisdiction. Canon 891 of itself does not confer this jurisdiction on the Novice Master or his *Socius*. (pp. 115-118)

14. The catechetical instruction which the Novice Master is to give to the lay novices must be a special instruction over and above the general instruction or conference given daily to all the novices in common. (p. 127)

15. In clerical religious Orders and Congregations this special catechetical instruction must be given to the lay novices. In lay religious Institutes it must be given to all the postulants and *all* the novices, whether they be choir or lay novices. (pp. 128-129)

16. The formal pursuit of studies is forbidden in the novitiate. But a moderate amount of study to review subjects previously pursued seems permissible, according to the norms of the instruction of 1910 of the Sacred Congregation of Religious. (p. 133)

17. During the second year of novitiate, if such is required, the novices may be engaged in the occupations of the Institute only if the constitutions prescribe it, and provided that the fundamental laws of the novitiate are not transgressed. The novices may be so engaged only moderately, and solely for their own instruction. They may never be so employed primarily for the benefit of the community. (pp. 136-137)

BIBLIOGRAPHY

Sources

Acta Apostolicae Sedis, Commentarium Officiale, Romae, 1909-1929; Civitate Vaticana, 1929—.

Acta Sanctae Sedis, 41 vols., Romae, 1865-1908.

Bruns, H. T., *Canones Apostolorum et Conciliorum Saeculorum IV-VII,* 2 vols., Berolini, 1839.

Bullarum Diplomatum et Privilegiorum Sanctorum Romanorum Pontificum Taurinensis editio, 25 vols., Augustae Taurinorum, 1857-1872.

Bullarium Ordinis FF. Praedicatorum, 8 vols., Romae, 1729-1740.

Butler, Cuthbert, *Sancti Benedicti Regula Monasteriorum, Editio Critico-Practica,* 2. ed., Friburgi Brisgoviae, 1927.

Canones et Decreta Sacrosancti et Oecumenici Concilii Tridentini, Editio Novissima ad Fidem Optimorum Exemplarium castigate Impressa, XIX Reimpressio Stereotypa, Taurini, 1913.

Codex Iuris Canonici Pii X Pontificis Maximi iussu digestus Benedicti XV auctoritate promulgatus, Romae: Typis Polyglottis Vaticanis, 1917.

Codex Iuris Canonici Fontes, cura Emi Card. Gasparri editi, 9 vols., Romae (postea Civitate Vaticana): Typis Polyglottis Vaticanis, 1923-1939. (Vols. VII, VIII, et IX cura et studio Emi Iustiniani Card. Serédi.)

Collectanea in usum secretariae Sacrae Congregationis Episcoporum et Regularium, ed. A. Bizzarri, Romae, 1863.

Corpus Iuris Canonici, editio Lipsiensis secunda post Aemilii Ludovici Richteri curas ad librorum manu scriptorum et editionis Romanae fidem recognovit et adnotatione critica instruxit Aemilius Friedberg, Lipsiae, 1879-1881.

Corpus Scriptorum Ecclesiasticorum Latinorum, Vindobonae, 1866—.

Decretum Gratiani Emendatum et Notationibus Illustratum una cum glossis, Romae, 1582.

Decretales D. Gregorii Papae IX, una cum glossis restitutae, Romae, 1582.

Jaffé, Phillipus, *Regesta Pontificum Romanorum, ab condita ecclesia ad annum post Christum natum 1198,* 2. ed., correctam et auctam auspiciis Gulielmi Wattenbach curaverunt S. Loewenfeld, F. Kaltenbrunner, P. Ewald, 2 vols. in 1, Lipsiae, 1885-1888.

Mansi, Joannes, *Sacrorum Conciliorum Nova et Amplissima Collectio,* 53 vols. in 60, Parisiis, Arnhem, Lipsiae, 1901-1927.

Monumenta Germaniae Historica, Inde ab anno Christi quingentesimo usque ad annum millesimum et quingentesimum edidit Societas Aperiendis Fontibus Rerum Germanicarum Medii Aevi, *Legum Sectio III,* Tom. II (*Concilia*), Pars I, ed. A. Werminghoff, Hannoverae, 1906.

Normae secundum quas S. Congregatio Episcoporum et Regularium procedere solet in Approbandis novis Institutis votorum simplicium, Romae: Typis S.C. de Propaganda Fide, 1901.

Pallottini, Salvator, *Collectio Omnium Conclusionum et Resolutionum Quae in Causis Propositis apud Sacram Congregationem Cardinalium S. Concilii Tridentini Interpretum Prodierunt ab eius Institutione Anno MCLXIV ad MDCCCLX, Distinctis Titulis Alphabetico Ordine per Materias Digesta,* 18 vols., Romae, 1868-1895.

Authors

Aichner, Simon, *Compendium Juris Ecclesiastici,* 6. ed., Brixinae, 1887.

Alphonsus Liguori, St., *Theologia Moralis,* ed. L. Gaudé, 4 vols., Romae, 1905-1912.

Altaner, Berthold, *Patrologie,* Freiburg im Breisgau: Herder, 1938.

Arndt, Augustin, *Die kirchlichen Rechtsbestimmungen für die Frauen-Congregationen,* Mainz, 1901.

Bargilliat, M., *Praelectiones Juris Canonici,* 28. ed., 2 vols., Parisiis, 1913.

Bastien, Pierre, *Directoire Canonique a l'usage des Congrégations à voeux simples,* 1. ed., Bruges, 1904; 4. ed., Bruges, 1933.

Battandier, Albert, *Guide canonique pour les constitutions des instituts à voeux simples,* 6. ed., Paris, 1923.

Berlière, Ursmer, *L'ordre monastique des Origines au XIIe siècle,* 3. ed., Paris, 1924.

Berutti, Christophorus, *Institutiones Iuris Canonici,* 6 vols., Vol. III *De Religiosis,* Taurini-Romae: Marietti, 1936.

Beste, Udalricus, *Introductio in Codicem,* 2. ed., Collegeville, Minn.: St. John's Abbey Press, 1944.

Biederlack, Josephus-Führich, Maximilianus, *De Religiosis,* Oeniponte, 1919.

Blat, Albertus, *Commentarium Textus Codicis Iuris Canonici,* 5 vols. in 6, 1919-1927; Lib. II, *Ius de Religiosis,* 3. ed., 1938, Romae: Apud "Angelicum."

Brandys, Maximillian, *Kirchliches Rechtsbuch,* 2. ed., Paderborn, 1920.

Butler, Cuthbert, *Benedictine Monachism,* 2. ed., London: Longmans, Green and Co., 1924.

———, *The Lausiac History of Palladius,* Texts and Studies, Cambridge, 1898.

Cabrol, Fernand, et Leclercq, Henri, *Dictionnaire d'archéologie chrétienne et de liturgie,* 14 vols., Paris: Librairie Letouzey et Ané, 1907—.

Cappello, Felix, *Summa Iuris Canonici,* 3 vols., Romae: Apud Aedes Universitatis Gregorianae, 1928-1936.

———, *Tractatus Canonico-Moralis de Sacramentis,* 3 vols. in 5, Taurinorum Augustae: Marietti, Vol. I, 2. ed., 1928; Vol. II, pars I, *De Poenitentia,* 2. ed., 1929.

Castropalao, Ferdinandus de, *Opus Morale de Virtutibus et Vitiis Contrariis,* 7 vols. in 3, Lugduni, 1700.

Chelodi, Ioannes-Ciprotti, Pius, *Ius Canonicum de Personis,* 3. ed., Vincenza: Societá Anonima Tipografica, 1942.

Cicognani, Amleto, *Canon Law,* Philadelphia: Dolphin Press, 1934.

Claeys Bouuaert, F.-Simenon, G., *Manuale Juris Canonici,* 3 vols., Vols. I et III, 3. ed., Gandae et Leodii: De Meester, 1930-1931.

Cocchi, Guidus, *Commentarium in Codicem Iuris Canonici,* 8 vols. in 5, Lib. II, *De Personis,* Pars II, Taurinorum Augustae: Marietti, 1924.

Coronata, Matthaeus Conte a, *Institutiones Iuris Canonici,* 5 vols., Vols. I-II, 2. ed., 1939; Vols. III-V, 1933-1936, Taurini: Marietti.

———, *De Sacramentis*—Tractatus Canonicus, 3 vols., Taurini: Marietti, 1943-1946.

Creusen, Joseph-Garesché, Edward-Ellis, Adam, *Religious Men and Women in the Code,* 3. ed., Milwaukee: Bruce, 1940.

Daoyz, Stephanus, *Iuris Pontificii Index et Summa,* 4 vols. in 2, Burdigalae, 1623.

De Angelis, P., *Praelectiones Iuris Canonici,* 2. ed., 5 vols., Romae, 1908.

De Meester, Alphonsus, *Juris Canonici et Juris Canonico-Civilis Compendium,* ed. nova, 3 vols. in 4, Brugis: Desclée, 1921-1928.

Donatus, Hyacintus, *Rerum Regularium Praxis Resolutoria,* 4 vols. in 2, Coloniae Agrippinae, 1728.

Evans, Joan, *Monastic Life at Cluny 910-1157,* London: Oxford University Press, 1931.

Fanfani, Ludovicus, *De Iure Religiosorum,* 2. ed., Taurini-Romae: Marietti, 1925.

Ferraris, Lucius, *Prompta Bibliotheca, Canonica, Iuridica, Moralis, Theologica, necnon Ascetica, Polemica, Rubricistica, Historica,* 8 vols., Romae, 1757-1762.

Ferreres, Joannes, *Institutiones Canonicae,* 2. ed., 2 vols., Barcinone, 1920.

Franco, Secondo, *Direction de Conscience,* Lettre a une Superieure Religieuse, trans. A-E. Gautier, 4. ed., Paris: Téqui, 1936.

Freriks, Celestine, *Religious Congregations in their External Relations,* The Catholic University of America Canon Law Studies, n. 1, Washington, D. C.: The Catholic University of America, 1916.

Galbraith, G. R., *The Constitution of the Dominican Order,* Manchester: The University Press, 1925.

Gerster a Zeil, Thomas, *Ius Religiosorum,* Taurini: Marietti, 1935.

Giraldi, Ubaldus, *Expositio Iuris Pontificii,* 2 vols., Romae, 1769.

Grandclaude, E., *Jus Canonicum,* 3 vols., Parisiis, 1882.

Haeften, Benedict von, *S. Benedictus illustratus, sive disquisitionum monasticarum libri XII, quibus S. P. Benedicti regula religiosorum rituum antiquitates varie dilucidantur,* Antverpiae, 1644.

Hefele, Carolus-Leclercq, Henricus, *Histoire des Conciles,* 10 vols. in 19, Paris: Librairie Letouzey et Ané, 1907-1938.

Huber, Raphael, *A Documented History of the Franciscan Order 1182-1517,* Milwaukee: The Nowiny Publishing Apostolate, 1944.

Iorio, Thomas, *Theologia Moralis*, 6. ed., 3 vols., Neapoli: D'Auria, 1938-1939.

Jansen, Joseph, *Ordensrecht*, 2. ed., Paderborn: Schöningh, 1920; 3. ed., 1931.

Jardi, Antonio, *El Derecho de las Religiosas*, 2. ed., Vich: Typografía Franciscana, 1927.

Kenney, James, *The Sources for the Early History of Ireland*, 2 vols., New York: Columbia University Press, 1929.

Knowles, David, *The Monastic Order in England*, Cambridge: The University Press, 1940.

Ladeuze, Paulin, *Étude sur le Cénobitisme Pakhomien pendant le IVe Siècle et la première moitié du Ve*, Paris, 1898.

Lanslots, D., *Handbook of Canon Law for Congregations of Women under Simple Vows*, 5. ed., New York: Pustet, 1911.

Lehmkuhl, Augustinus, *Theologia Moralis*, 10. ed., 2 vols., Friburgi Brisgoviae, 1902.

Lessius, Leonardus, *De Iustitia et Iure Caeterisque Virtutibus Cardinalibus*, 4 vols. in 1, Lugduni, 1653.

Marc, Clemens-Gestermann, Franciscus, *Institutiones Morales Alphonsianae*, 17. ed., 2 vols., Lugduni: Vitte, 1922-1923; 9. ed., Romae, 1898.

Martène, Edmond, *De Antiquis Ecclesiae Ritibus*, 4 vols. in 3, Rotomagi, 1700-1702.

———, *Veterum scriptorum et monumentorum moralium, historicorum, dogmaticorum collectio nova*, Paris, 1700.

Meynard, André, *Réponses canoniques et pratiques de religieuses à voeux simples*, 2. ed., Paris, 1891.

Michiels, Gommarus, *Normae Generales Juris Canonici*, 2 vols., Lublin: Universitas Catholica, 1929.

Migne, P. J., *Patrologiae Cursus Completus*, Series Latina, 221 vols., Parisiis, 1844-1864.

———, *Patrologiae Cursus Completus*, Series Graeca, 161 vols., Parisiis, 1856-1866.

Molitor, Raphael, *Religiosi Iuris Capita Selecta*, Ratisbonae, 1909.

Montalembert, Le Comte de, *Les Moines d'Occident*, 6. ed., 7 vols., Parisiis, 1878-1882.

———, *Saint Columban*, critical edition: E. J. McCarthy, St. Columbans, Nebraska, 1927.

McCormick, Robert, *Confessors of Religious*, The Catholic University of America Canon Law Studies, n. 33, Washington, D. C.: The Catholic University of America, 1926.

McLaughlin, Terence, *Le très ancien droit monastique de l'Occident*, Paris: Picard, 1935.

Nervegna, Josephus, *De Jure Practico Regularium*, Romae, 1900.

Ojetti, Benedictus, *Synopsis Rerum Moralium et Juris Pontificii*, 3. ed., 4 vols., Romae, 1909-1914.

Ottaviani, Alaphridus, *Institutiones Iuris Publici Ecclesiastici*, 2. ed., 2 vols., Romae: Typis Polyglottis Vaticanis, 1935-1936.

Papi, Hector, *Religious in Church Law,* New York: Kenedy, 1924.

Pejška, Josephus, *Ius Canonicum Religiosorum,* 3. ed., Friburgi Brisgoviae: Herder, 1927.

Piatus Montensis (J. J. Loiseaux), *Praelectiones Juris Regularis,* 3. ed., 2 vols., Tornaci, 1906.

Pirhing, Ernricus, *Compendium Juris Canonici,* Dilingae, 1690.

Prümmer, Dominicus, *Manuale Iuris Canonici,* 5. ed., Friburgi Brisgoviae: Herder, 1927.

Raus, J. B., *De Sacrae Obedientiae Virtute et Voto,* Lugduni: Vitte, 1923.

———, *Institutiones Canonicae,* 2. ed., Lugduni-Parisiis: Vitte, 1931.

Raymundus de Pennaforte, St., *Summa,* ed. nova, Veronae, 1744.

Reiffenstuel, Anacletus, *Jus Canonicum Universum,* 5 vols. in 3, Venetiis, 1760.

Ryan, John, *Irish Monasticism,* London: Longmans, Green and Co., 1931.

Salmanticensis Collegii Cursus Theologiae Moralis, 6 vols. in 4, Vols. I-II, 6. ed., 1722; Vols. III-IV, ed. novissima, 1714; Vol. V, 1725; Vol. VI, 1724, Venetiis.

Santi, Franciscus-Leitner, Martinus, *Praelectiones Juris Canonici,* 4. ed., 3 vols., Ratisbonae, 1903-1905.

Schaefer, Timotheus, *De Religiosis ad Normam Codicis Iuris Canonici,* 3. ed., Romae: S.A.L.E.R., 1940.

Schmalzgrueber, Franciscus, *Jus Ecclesiasticum Universum,* 5 vols. in 3, Neapoli, 1738.

Schroeder, H., *Disciplinary Decrees of the General Councils,* St. Louis: B. Herder Book Co., 1937.

Sebastianelli, Guilelmus, *Praelectiones Juris Canonici,* 2. ed., 3 vols., Romae, 1905-1906.

Sipos, Stephanus, *Enchiridion Iuris Canonici,* Pécs: Ex Typographia "Haladas R.T.," 1926.

Suarez, Franciscus, *Opera Omnia,* 28 vols., Parisiis, 1856-1878; Vols. XV, XVI, *De Religione,* 1859, 1860.

Thomas Aquinas, St., *Doctoris Angelici Opera Omnia Iussu Impensaque Leonis XIII, P.M. Edita,* Romae, 1882—.

———, *Summa Theologica,* Romae, 1888-1906.

Thomassinus, Ludovicus, *Vetus et Nova Ecclesiae Disciplina,* 3 vols., Venetiis, 1730.

Toso, Albertus, *Ad Codicem Juris Canonici Commentaria Minora,* 5 vols. in 2, Romae: Marietti, 1921-1927.

Valuy, B., *Le gouvernement des communautés religieuses,* 2. ed., Paris, 1866.

Van Espen, Zegerus, *Jus Ecclesiasticum Universum,* 5 vols. in 2, Coloniae Agrippinae, 1729.

Van Hove, A., *De Legibus Ecclesiasticis,* Mechliniae-Romae: Dessain, 1930.

Vasquez, G., *Commentaria ac Disputationes in tertiam partem Sancti Thomae,* 4 vols., Lugduni, 1631.

Vermeersch, Arthurus, *De Religiosis Institutis et Personis,* 1. ed., 2 vols., Romae, 1902; 2. ed., 1907; 4. ed., 1909.

———, *Theologiae Moralis Principia, Responsa, Consilia,* 2. ed., 4 vols., Brugis: Beyaert, 1926-1928.

Vermeersch, Arthurus-Creusen, Josephus, *Epitome Iuris Canonici,* 3. ed., 3 vols., Mechliniae-Romae: Dessain, 1927-1928; 5. ed., 1933-1936.

Vito, Pasquale, *De Religiosis,* Napoli: Pontificia Facoltà Giuridica di Napoli, 1943.

Wernz, Franciscus, *Ius Decretalium,* 2. ed., 6 vols., Romae et Prati, 1906-1913.

Wernz, Franciscus-Vidal, Petrus, *Ius Canonicum,* 7 vols. in 8, Romae: Universitas Gregoriana, 1923-1938.

Articles

Anonymous, "Manifestation of Conscience and Chapter of Faults"—*AER,* XX (1899), 420-421.

———, "Dying Postulants Cannot Be Admitted to Profession"—*AER,* C (1939), 447-452.

Berutti, C., "De Confessariis Religiosorum"—*JP,* XIII (1933), 73-87.

Ciprotti, P., "Adhuc de seminarii rectore an ordinariam iurisdictionem habeat ad alumnorum confessiones audiendas"—*Apollinaris,* VIII (1935), 609-610.

De Langogne, P., "De la profession religieuse anticipée *in articulo mortis*"—*Le Canoniste Contemporain,* XVIII (1895), 1-9.

———, "Le nouveau décret de la S.C. des Évêques et Réguliers et l'ingérence des supérieurs et supérieures dans le for de la conscience"—*Le Canoniste Contemporain,* XIV (1891), 69-78; 109-115; 156-165; 205-213; 244-255.

Führich, M., "Das Ordensrecht nach dem *Codex Iuris Canonici*"—*TPQ,* LXXII (1919), 170-182; 370-390.

Goyeneche, S., "De Transitu ad aliam Religionem"—*CpR,* II (1921), 116-124.

———, "Annotationes"—*CpR,* IV (1923), 260-265.

———, "Consultationes"—*CpR,* I (1920), 51-52; IV (1923), 340-341; V (1924), 165-166; VI (1925), 486-491; VII (1926), 41-42; VIII (1927), 115-117; XII (1931), 254; XIII (1932), 39-40; XIV (1933), 356; *CpRM,* XVIII (1937), 90-95, 157-158; XX (1939), 18-19, 310-311; XXIII (1942), 18-21, 265-267.

Hofmeister, P., "*Professio in articulo mortis* unter dem neuen Recht"—*TPQ,* LXXIV (1921), 493-500.

Kinane, J., "The Confessor of Novices in Religious Institutes of Men"—*IER,* 5. series, XLI (1933), 87-88.

Kraemer, P., "De professione religiosa a novitio in mortis articulo vel periculo constituto emittenda"—*Periodica,* XXXI (1942), 140-142.

Larraona, A., "Commentarium Codicis"—*CpR,* XII (1931), 124-130; *CpRM,* XVI (1935), 307-312; XXIII (1942), 251-264; XXIV (1943), 25-40, 116-124, 199-216; XXV (1946), 3-20.

———, "Consultationes"—*CpR,* I (1920), 51-52; II (1921), 291-299.

Maroto, P., "Annotationes"—*CpR,* I (1920), 106-107; *CpR,* III (1922), 38-44; X (1929), 334-341; *CpRM,* XVI (1935), 371-376.

Oesterle, G., "De relationibus inter metum gravem et invaliditatem novitiatus et professionis"—*CpR,* XV (1934), 386-411.

Prikryl, F., "Ein sonderbares Noviziat"—*TPQ,* XCI (1938), 112-116.

Ramos, D., "De conditione saecularium in domibus religiosorum"—*CpR,* VI (1925), 187-190.

Vermeersch, A., "De quibusdam postulantibus in religiosas familias non admittendis"—*Periodica,* V (1913), 53-56.

———, "De aliqua in noviciatu studiis opera danda"—*Periodica,* V (1913), 195-197.

———, "De professione novicii vel probandi in articulo mortis"—*Periodica,* XII (1923), (159)-(162).

Voltas, P., "De aperienda, directionis causa, superioribus conscientia"—*CpR,* I (1920), 83-92; 117-125; 145-151.

———, "Consultatio"—*CpR,* II (1921), 220-221.

Periodicals

Acta Ordinis Minorum, Romae, 1882-1886; Florentiae, 1887—.

American Ecclesiastical Review, The (formerly *Ecclesiastical Review, The,* July, 1905-December, 1943), Philadelphia, 1889-1943; Washington, 1944—.

Analecta Ecclesiastica, Romae, 1893-1911.

Analecta Juris Pontificii, Romae, 1855-1869; Parisiis, 1872-1891.

Apollinaris, Romae, 1928—.

Commentarium pro Religiosis (later [1935] *Commentarium pro Religiosis et Missionariis*), Romae, 1920—.

Il Monitore Ecclesiastico, Romae, 1876—.

Irish Ecclesiastical Record, The, Dublin, 1864—.

Jus Pontificium, Romae, 1921—.

Le Canoniste Contemporain, Paris, 1878-1922.

Periodica de Re Canonica et Morali utili praesertim Religiosis et Missionariis, Brugis, 1905—.

Theologisch-praktische Quartalschrift, Linz, 1832—.

Zeitschrift für Kirchengeschichte, Gotha, 1880—.

ABBREVIATIONS

AAS—Acta Apostolicae Sedis.
AER—American Ecclesiastical Review, The.
AJP—Analecta Juris Pontificii.
ASS—Acta Sanctae Sedis.
Bull. Rom.—Bullarum Romanum.
CpR—Commentarium pro Religiosis.
CpRM—Commentarium pro Religiosis et Missionariis.
Fontes—Codicis Iuris Canonici Fontes.
IER—Irish Ecclesiastical Record, The.
JP—Jus Pontificium.
Normae—Normae secundum quas S.C. Ep. et Reg. procedere solet in approbandis novis Institutis votorum simplicium.
Periodica—Periodica de Re Canonica et Morali.
TPQ—Theologisch-praktische Quartalschrift.

ALPHABETICAL INDEX

BIOGRAPHICAL NOTE

James Francis Lover was born on November 26, 1916, in Brooklyn, New York. After completing his elementary education in the parochial school of Our Lady of Perpetual Help, Brooklyn, New York, he entered St. Mary's College, the Juvenate of the Redemptorist Fathers at North East, Pennsylvania, in August, 1930. On August 1, 1936, he received the habit of the Congregation of the Most Holy Redeemer at Ilchester, Maryland, and made his religious profession on August 2nd of the following year. His seminary course was made at the Redemptorist House of Studies, Mount St. Alphonsus, Esopus, New York, where he was ordained to the priesthood on June 21, 1942. In September of 1943 he entered the Catholic University of America to pursue a graduate course of studies in the School of Social Sciences. He received the Master of Arts Degree in Sociology, in May, 1944. He then enrolled in the School of Canon Law, from which he received the Baccalaureate in Canon Law in May, 1945, and the Licentiate in Canon Law in June, 1946.

CANON LAW STUDIES *

1. Freriks, Rev. Celestine A., C.PP.S., J.C.D., Religious Congregations in Their External Relations, 121 pp., 1916.
2. Galliher, Rev. Daniel M., O.P., J.C.D., Canonical Elections, 117 pp., 1917.
3. Borkowski, Rev. Aurelius L., O.F.M., J.C.D., De Confraternitatibus Ecclesiasticis, 136 pp., 1918.
4. Castillo, Rev. Cayo, J.C.D., Disertacion Historico-Canonica sobre la Potestad del Cabildo en Sede Vacante o Impedida del Vicario Capitular, 99 pp., 1919 (1918).
5. Kubelbeck, Rev. William J., S.T.B., J.C.D., The Sacred Penitentiaria and Its Relation to Faculties of Ordinaries and Priests, 129 pp., 1918.
6. Petrovits, Rev. Joseph, J.C., S.T.D., J.C.D., The New Church Law on Matrimony, X-461 pp., 1919.
7. Hickey, Rev. John J., S.T.B., J.C.D., Irregularities and Simple Impediments in the New Code of Canon Law, 100 pp., 1920.
8. Klekotka, Rev. Peter J., S.T.B., J.C.D., Diocesan Consultors, 179 pp., 1920.
9. Wanenmacher, Rev. Francis, J.C.D., The Evidence in Ecclesiastical Procedure Affecting the Marriage Bond, 1920 (Printed 1935).
10. Golden, Rev. Henry Francis, J.C.D., Parochial Benefices in the New Code, IV-119 pp., 1921 (Printed 1925).
11. Koudelka, Rev. Charles J., J.C.D., Pastors, Their Rights and Duties According to the New Code of Canon Law, 211 pp., 1921.
12. Melo, Rev. Antonius, O.F.M., J.C.D., De Exemptione Regularium, X-188 pp., 1921.
13. Schaaf, Rev. Valentine Theodore, O.F.M., S.T.B., J.C.D., The Cloister. X-180 pp., 1921.
14. Burke, Rev. Thomas Joseph, S.T.D., J.C.D., Competence in Ecclesiastical Tribunals, IV-117 pp., 1922.
15. Leech, Rev. George Leo, J.C.D., A Comparative Study of the Constitution "Apostolicae Sedis" and the "Codex Juris Canonici," 179 pp., 1922.
16. Motry, Rev. Hubert Louis, S.T.D., J.C.D., Diocesan Faculties According to the Code of Canon Law, II-167 pp., 1922.
17. Murphy, Rev. George Lawrence, J.C.D., Delinquencies and Penalties in the Administration and the Reception of the Sacraments, IV-121 pp., 1923.
18. O'Reilly, Rev. John Anthony, S.T.B., J.C.D., Ecclesiastical Sepulture in the New Code of Canon Law, II-129 pp., 1923.

---

* From nn. 1-100 inclusive only n. 25 is still obtainable.

From n. 101 onward all numbers are available except the following: nn. 101-114 inclusive, and also nn. 116, 118, 120, 122, 123 and 162.

19. Michalicka, Rev. Wenceslas Cyrill, O.S.B., J.C.D., Judicial Procedure in Dismissal of Clerical Exempt Religious, 107 pp., 1923.

20. Dargin, Rev. Edward Vincent, S.T.B., J.C.D., Reserved Cases According to the Code of Canon Law, IV-103 pp., 1924.

21. Godfrey, Rev. John A., S.T.B., J.C.D., The Right of Patronage According to the Code of Canon Law, 153 pp., 1924.

22. Hagedorn, Rev. Francis Edward, J.C.D., General Legislation on Indulgences, II-154 pp., 1924.

23. King, Rev. James Ignatius, J.C.D., The Administration of the Sacraments to Dying Non-Catholics, V-141 pp., 1924.

24. Winslow, Rev. Francis Joseph, O.F.M., J.C.D., Vicars and Prefects Apostolic, IV-149 pp., 1924.

25. Correa, Rev. Jose Servelion, S.T.L., J.C.D., La Potestad Legislativa de la Iglesia Catolica, IV-127 pp., 1925.

26. Dugan, Rev. Henry Francis, A.M., J.C.D., The Judiciary Department of the Diocesan Curia, 87 pp., 1925.

27. Keller, Rev. Charles Frederick, S.T.B., J.C.D., Mass Stipends, 167 pp., 1925.

28. Paschang, Rev. John Linus, J.C.D., The Sacramentals According to the Code of Canon Law, 129 pp., 1925.

29. Piontek, Rev. Cyrillus, O.F.M., S.T.B., J.C.D., De Indulto Exclaustrationis necnon Saecularizationis, XIII-289 pp., 1925.

30. Kearney, Rev. Richard Joseph, S.T.B., J.C.D., Sponsors at Baptism According to the Code of Canon Law, IV-127 pp., 1925.

31. Bartlett, Rev. Chester Joseph, A.M., LL.B., J.C.D., The Tenure of Parochial Property in the United States of America, V-108 pp., 1926.

32. Kilker, Rev. Adrian Jerome, J.C.D., Extreme Unction, V-425 pp., 1926.

33. McCormick, Rev. Robert Emmett, J.C.D., Confessors of Religious, VIII-266 pp., 1926.

34. Miller, Rev. Newton Thomas, J.C.D., Founded Masses According to the Code of Canon Law, VII-93 pp., 1926.

35. Roelker, Rev. Edward G., S.T.D., J.C.D., Principles of Privilege According to the Code of Canon Law, XI-166 pp., 1926.

36. Bakalarczyk, Rev. Richardus, M.I.C., J.U.D., De Novitiatu, VIII-208 pp., 1927.

37. Pizzuti, Rev. Lawrence, O.F.M., J.U.L., De Parochis Religiosis, 1927. (Not Printed.)

38. Bliley, Rev. Nicholas Martin, O.S.B., J.C.D., Altars According to the Code of Canon Law, XIX-132 pp., 1927.

39. Brown, Mr. Brendan Francis, A.B., LL.M., J.U.D., The Canonical Juristic Personality with Special Reference to its Status in the United States of America, V-212 pp., 1927.

40. Cavanaugh, Rev. William Thomas, C.P., J.U.D., The Reservation of the Blessed Sacrament, VIII-101 pp., 1927.

41. Doheny, Rev. William J., C.S.C., A.B., J.C.D., Church Property: Modes of Acquisition, X-118 pp., 1927.
42. Feldhaus, Rev. Aloysius H., C.PP.S., J.C.D., Oratories, IX-141 pp., 1927
43. Kelly, Rev. James Patrick, A.B., J.C.D., The Jurisdiction of the Simple Confessor, X-208 pp., 1927.
44. Neuberger, Rev. Nicholas J., J.C.D., Canon 6 or the Relation of the Codex Juris Canonici to the Preceding Legislation, V-95 pp., 1927.
45. O'Keefe, Rev. Gerald Michael, J.C.D., Matrimonial Dispensations. Powers of Bishops, Priests, and Confessors, VIII-232 pp., 1927.
46. Quigley, Rev. Joseph A. M., A.B., J.C.D., Condemned Societies, 139 pp., 1927.
47. Zaplotnik, Rev. Johannes Leo, J.C.D., De Vicariis Foraneis, X-142 pp., 1927.
48. Duskie, Rev. John Aloysius, A.B., J.C.D., The Canonical Status of the Orientals in the United States, VIII-196 pp., 1928.
49. Hyland, Rev. Francis Edward, J.C.D., Excommunication, Its Nature, Historical Development and Effects, VIII-181 pp., 1928.
50. Reinmann, Rev. Gerald Joseph, O.M.C., J.C.D., The Third Order Secular of Saint Francis, 201 pp., 1928.
51. Schenk, Rev. Francis J., J.C.D., The Matrimonial Impediments of Mixed Religion and Disparity of Cult, XVI-318 pp., 1929.
52. Coady, Rev. John Joseph, S.T.D., J.U.D., A.M., The Appointment of Pastors, VIII-150 pp., 1929.
53. Kay, Rev. Thomas Henry, J.C.D., Competence in Matrimonial Procedure, VIII-164 pp., 1929.
54. Turner, Rev. Sidney Joseph, C.P., J.U.D., The Vow of Poverty, XLIX-217 pp., 1929.
55. Kearney, Rev. Raymond A., A.B., S.T.D., J.C.D., The Principles of Delegation, VII-149 pp., 1929.
56. Conran, Rev. Edward James, A.B., J.C.D., The Interdict, V-163 pp., 1930.
57. O'Neill, Rev. William H., J.C.D., Papal Rescripts of Favor, VII-218 pp., 1930.
58. Bastnagel, Rev. Clement Vincent, J.U.D., The Appointment of Parochial Adjutants and Assistants, XV-257 pp., 1930.
59. Ferry, Rev. William A., A.B., J.C.D., Stole Fees, V-136 pp., 1930.
60. Costello, Rev. John Michael, A.B., J.C.D., Domicile and Quasi-Domicile, VII-201 pp., 1930.
61. Kremer, Rev. Michael Nicholas, A.B., S.T.B., J.C.D., Church Support in the United States, VI-136 pp., 1930.
62. Angulo, Rev. Luis, C.M., J.C.D., Legislation de la Iglesia sobre la intencion en la application de la Santa Misa, VII-104 pp., 1931.
63. Frey, Rev. Wolfgang Norbert, O.S.B., A.B., J.C.D., The Act of Religious Profession, VIII-174 pp., 1931.

64. ROBERTS, REV. JAMES BRENDAN, A.B., J.C.D., The Banns of Marriage, XIV-140 pp., 1931.
65. RYDER, REV. RAYMOND ALOYSIUS, A.B., J.C.D., Simony, IX-151 pp., 1931.
66. CAMPAGNA, REV. ANGELO, PH.D., J.U.D., Il Vicario Generale del Vescovo, VII-205 pp., 1931.
67. COX, REV. JOSEPH GODFREY, A.B., J.C.D., The Administration of Seminaries, VI-124 pp., 1931.
68. GREGORY, REV. DONALD J., J.U.D., The Pauline Privilege, XV-165 pp., 1931.
69. DONOHUE, REV. JOHN F., J.C.D., The Impediment of Crime, VII-110 pp., 1931.
70. DOOLEY, REV. EUGENE A., O.M.I., J.C.D., Church Law on Sacred Relics, IX-143 pp., 1931.
71. ORTH, REV. CLEMENT RAYMOND, O.M.C., J.C.D., The Approbation of Religious Institutes, 171 pp., 1931.
72. PERNICONE, REV. JOSEPH M., A.B., J.C.D., The Ecclesiastical Prohibition of Books, XII-267 pp., 1932.
73. CLINTON, REV. CONNELL, A.B., J.C.D., The Paschal Precept, IX-108 pp., 1932.
74. DONNELLY, REV. FRANCIS B., A.M., S.T.L., J.C.D., The Diocesan Synod, VIII-125 pp., 1932.
75. TORRENTE, REV. CAMILO, C.M.F., J.C.D., Las Procesiones Sagradas, V-145 pp., 1932.
76. MURPHY, REV. EDWIN J., C.PP.S., J.C.D., Suspension Ex Informata Conscientia, XI-122 pp., 1932.
77. MACKENZIE, REV. ERIC F., A.M., S.T.L., J.C.D., The Delict of Heresy in its Commission, Penalization, Absolution, VII-124 pp., 1932.
78. LYONS, REV. AVITUS E., S.T.B., J.C.D., The Collegiate Tribunal of First Instance, XI-147 pp., 1932.
79. CONNOLLY, REV. THOMAS A., J.C.D., Appeals, XI-195, pp., 1932.
80. SANGMEISTER, REV. JOSEPH V., A.B., J.C.D., Force and Fear as Precluding Matrimonial Consent, V-211 pp., 1932.
81. JAEGER, REV. LEO A., A.B., J.C.D., The Administration of Vacant and Quasi-Vacant Episcopal Sees in the United States, IX-229 pp., 1932.
82. RIMLINGER, REV. HERBERT T., J.C.D., Error Invalidating Matrimonial Consent, VII-79 pp., 1932.
83. BARRETT, REV. JOHN D. M., S.S., J.C.D., A Comparative Study of the Councils of Baltimore and the Code of Canon Law, IX-223 pp., 1932.
84. CARBERRY, REV. JOHN J., PH.D., S.T.D., J.C.D., The Juridical Form of Marriage, X-177 pp., 1934.
85. DOLAN, REV. JOHN L., A.B., J.C.D., The Defensor Vinculi, XII-157 pp., 1934.
86. HANNAN, REV. JEROME D., A.M., S.T.D., LL.B., J.C.D., The Canon Law of Wills, IX-517 pp., 1934.

87. LEMIEUX, REV. DELISE A., A.M., J.C.D., The Sentence in Ecclesiastical Procedure, IX-131 pp., 1934.
88. O'ROURKE, REV. JAMES J., A.B., J.C.D., Parish Registers, VII-109 pp., 1934.
89. TIMLIN, REV. BARTHOLOMEW, O.F.M., A.M., J.C.D., Conditional Matrimonial Consent, X-381 pp., 1934.
90. WAHL, REV. FRANCIS X., A.B., J.C.D., The Matrimonial Impediments of Consanguinity and Affinity, VI-125 pp., 1934.
91. WHITE, REV. ROBERT J., A.B., LL.B., S.T.B., J.C.D., Canonical Ante-Nuptial Promises and the Civil Law, VI-152 pp., 1934.
92. HERRERA, REV. ANTONIO PARRA, O.C.D., J.C.D., Legislacion Ecclesiastica sobra el Ayuno y la Abstinencia, XI-191 pp., 1935.
93. KENNEDY, REV. EDWIN J., J.C.D., The Special Matrimonial Process in Cases of Evident Nullity, X-165 pp., 1935.
94. MANNING, REV. JOHN J., A.B., J.C.D., Presumption of Law in Matrimonial Procedure, XI-111 pp., 1935.
95. MOEDER, REV. JOHN M., J.C.D., The Proper Bishop for Ordination and Dismissorial Letters, VII-135 pp., 1935.
96. O'MARA, REV. WILLIAM A., A.B., J.C.D., Canonical Causes for Matrimonial Dispensations, IX-155 pp., 1935.
97. REILLY, REV. PETER, J.C.D., Residence of Pastors, IX-81 pp., 1935.
98. SMITH, REV. MARINER T., O.P., S.T.Lr., J.C.D., The Penal Law for Religious, VIII-169 pp., 1935.
99. WHALEN, REV. DONALD W., A.M., J.C.D., The Value of Testimonial Evidence in Matrimonial Procedure, XIII-297 pp., 1935.
100. CLEARY, REV. JOSEPH F., J.C.D., Canonical Limitations on the Alienation of Church Property, VIII-141 pp., 1936.
101. GLYNN, REV. JOHN C., J.C.D., The Promoter of Justice, XX-337 pp., 1936.
102. BRENNAN, REV. JAMES H., S.S., M.A., S.T.B., J.C.D., The Simple Convalidation of Marriage, VI-135 pp., 1937.
103. BRUNINI, REV. JOSEPH BERNARD, J.C.D., The Clerical Obligations of Canons 139 and 142, X-121 pp., 1937.
104. CONNOR, REV. MAURICE, A.B., J.C.D., The Administrative Removal of Pastors, VIII-159 pp., 1937.
105. GUILFOYLE, REV. MERLIN JOSEPH, J.C.D., Custom, XI-144 pp., 1937.
106. HUGHES, REV. JAMES AUSTIN, A.B., A.M., J.C.D., Witnesses in Criminal Trials of Clerics, IX-140 pp., 1937.
107. JANSEN, REV. RAYMOND J., A.B., S.T.L., J.C.D., Canonical Provisions for Catechetical Instruction, VII-153 pp., 1937.
108. KEALY, REV. JOHN JAMES, A.B., J.C.D., The Introductory Libellus in Church Court Procedure, XI-121 pp., 1937.
109. MCMANUS, REV. JAMES EDWARD, C.SS.R., J.C.D., The Administration of Temporal Goods in Religious Institutes, XVI-196 pp., 1937.

110. Moriarty, Rev. Eugene James, J.C.D., Oaths in Ecclesiastical Courts, X-115 pp., 1937.
111. Rainer, Rev. Eligius George, C.SS.R., J.C.D., Suspension of Clerics, XVII-249 pp., 1937.
112. Reilly, Rev. Thomas F., C.SS.R., J.C.D., Visitation of Religious, VI-195 pp., 1938.
113. Moriarty, Rev. Francis E., C.SS.R., J.C.D., The Extraordinary Absolution from Censures, XV-334 pp., 1938.
114. Connolly, Rev. Nicholas P., J.C.D., The Canonical Erection of Parishes, X-132 pp., 1938.
115. Donovan, Rev. James Joseph, J.C.D., The Pastor's Obligation in Prenuptial Investigation, XII-322 pp., 1938.
116. Harrigan, Rev. Robert J., M.A., S.T.B., J.C.D., The Radical Sanation of Invalid Marriages, VIII-208 pp., 1938.
117. Boffa, Rev. Conrad Humbert, J.C.D., Canonical Provisions for Catholic Schools, VII-211 pp., 1939.
118. Parsons, Rev. Anscar John, O.M.Cap., J.C.D., Canonical Elections, XII-236 pp., 1939.
119. Reilly, Rev. Edward Michael, A.B., J.C.D., The General Norms of Dispensation, XII-156 pp., 1939.
120. Ryan, Rev. Gerald Aloysius, A.B., J.C.D., Principles of Episcopal Jurisdiction, XII-172 pp., 1939.
121. Burton, Rev. Francis James, C.S.C., A.B., J.C.D., A Commentary on Canon 1125, X-222 pp., 1940.
122. Miaskiewicz, Rev. Francis Sigismund, J.C.D., Supplied Jurisdiction According to Canon 209, XII-340 pp., 1940.
123. Rice, Rev. Patrick William, A.B., J.C.D., Proof of Death in Prenuptial Investigation, VIII-156 pp., 1940.
124. Anglin, Rev. Thomas Francis, M.S., J.C.D., The Eucharistic Fast, VIII-183 pp., 1941.
125. Coleman, Rev. John Jerome, J.C.D., The Minister of Confirmation, VI-153 pp., 1941.
126. Downs, Rev. John Emmanuel, A.B., J.C.D., The Concept of Clerical Immunity, XI-163 pp., 1941.
127. Esswein, Rev. Anthony Albert, J.C.D., Extrajudicial Penal Powers of Ecclesiastical Superiors, X-144 pp., 1941.
128. Farrell, Rev. Benjamin Francis, M.A., S.T.L., J.C.D., The Rights and Duties of the Local Ordinary Regarding Congregations of Women Religious of Pontifical Approval, V-195 pp., 1941.
129. Feeney, Rev. Thomas John, A.B., S.T.L., J.C.D., Restitutio in Integrum, VI-169 pp., 1941.
130. Findlay, Rev. Stephen William, O.S.B., A.B., J.C.D., Canonical Norms Governing the Deposition and Degradation of Clerics, XVII-279 pp., 1941.

131. Goodwine, Rev. John, A.B., S.T.L., J.C.D., The Right of the Church to Acquire Property, VIII-119 pp., 1941.
132. Heston, Rev. Edward Louis, C.S.C., Ph.D., S.T.D., J.C.D., The Alienation of Church Property in the United States, XII-222 pp., 1941.
133. Hogan, Rev. James John, A.B., S.T.L., J.C.D., Judicial Advocates and Procurators, XIII-200 pp., 1941.
134. Kealy, Rev. Thomas M., A.B., Litt.B., J.C.D., Dowry of Women Religious, IX-152 pp., 1941.
135. Keene, Rev. Michael James, O.S.B., J.C.D., Religious Ordinaries and Canon 198, V-164 pp., 1942.
136. Kerin, Rev. Charles A., S.S., M.A., S.T.B., J.C.D., The Privation of Christian Burial, XVI-279 pp., 1941.
137. Louis, Rev. William Francis, M.A., J.C.D., Diocesan Archives, X-101 pp., 1941.
138. McDevitt, Rev. Gilbert Joseph, A.B., J.C.D., Legitimacy and Legitimation, X-247 pp., 1941.
139. McDonough, Rev. Thomas Joseph, A.B., J.C.D., Apostolic Administrators, X-217 pp., 1941.
140. Meier, Rev. Carl Anthony, A.B., J.C.D., Penal Administrative Procedure Against Negligent Pastors, XI-240 pp., 1941.
141. Schmidt, Rev. John Rogg, A.B., J.C.D., The Principles of Authentic Interpretation in Canon 17 of the Code of Canon Law, XII-331 pp., 1941.
142. Slafkosky, Rev. Andrew Leonard, A.B., J.C.D., The Canonical Episcopal Visitation of the Diocese, X-197 pp., 1941.
143. Swoboda, Rev. Innocent Robert, O.F.M., J.C.D., Ignorance in Relation to the Imputability of Delicts, IX-271 pp., 1941.
144. Dubé, Rev. Arthur Joseph, A.B., J.C.D., The General Principles for the Reckoning of Time in Canon Law, VIII-299 pp., 1941.
145. McBride, Rev. James T., A.B., J.C.D., Incardination and Excardination of Seculars, XX-585 pp., 1941.
146. Król, Rev. John T., J.C.D., The Defendant in Ecclesiastical Trials, XII-207 pp., 1942.
147. Comyns, Rev. Joseph J., C.SS.R., A.B., J.C.D., Papal and Episcopal Administration of Church Property, XIV-155 pp., 1942.
148. Barry, Rev. Garrett Francis, O.M.I., J.C.D., Violation of the Cloister, XII-260 pp., 1942.
149. Bolduc, Rev. Gatien, C.S.V., A.B., S.T.L., J.C.D., Les Études dans les Religions Cléricales, VIII-155 pp., 1942.
150. Boyle, Rev. David John, M.A., J.C.D., The Juridic Effects of Moral Certitude on Pre-Nuptial Guarantees, XII-188 pp., 1942.
151. Canavan, Rev. Walter Joseph, M.A., Litt.D., J.C.D., The Profession of Faith, XII-143 pp., 1942.
152. Desrochers, Rev. Bruno, A.B., Ph.L., S.T.B., J.C.D., Le Premier Concile Plénier de Québec et le Code de Droit Canonique, XIV-186 pp., 1942.

153. DILLON, REV. ROBERT EDWARD, A.B., J.C.D., Common Law Marriage, X-148 pp., 1942.
154. DODWELL, REV. EDWARD JOHN, Ph.D., S.T.B., J.C.D., The Time and Place for the Celebration of Marriage, X-156 pp., 1942.
155. DONNELLAN, REV. THOMAS ANDREW, A.B., J.C.D., The Obligation of the Missa pro Populo, VII-131 pp., 1942.
156. ELTZ, REV. LOUIS ANTHONY, A.B., J.C.D., Cooperation in Crime, XII-208 pp., 1942.
157. GASS, REV. SYLVESTER FRANCIS, M.A., J.C.D., Ecclesiastical Pensions, XI-206 pp., 1942.
158. GUINIVEN, REV. JOHN JOSEPH, C.SS.R., J.C.D., The Precept of Hearing Mass, XIV-188 pp., 1942.
159. GULCZYNSKI, REV. JOHN THEOPHILUS, J.C.D., The Desecration and Violation of Churches, X-126 pp., 1942.
160. HAMMILL, REV. JOHN LEO, M.A., J.C.D., The Obligations of the Traveler According to Canon 14, VIII-204 pp., 1942.
161. HAYDT, REV. JOHN JOSEPH, A.B., J.C.D., Reserved Benefices, XI-148 pp., 1942.
162. HUSER, REV. ROGER JOHN, O.F.M., A.B., J.C.D., The Crime of Abortion in Canon Law, XII-187 pp., 1942.
163. KEARNEY, REV. FRANCIS PATRICK, A.B., S.T.L., J.C.D., The Principles of Canon 1127, X-162 pp., 1942.
164. LINAHEN, REV. LEO JAMES, S.T.L., J.C.D., De Absolutione Complicis in Peccato Turpi, V-114 pp., 1942.
165. McCLOSKEY, REV. JOSEPH ALOYSIUS, A.B., J.C.D., The Subject of Ecclesiastical Law According to Canon 12, XVII-246 pp., 1942.
166. O'NEILL, REV. FRANCIS JOSEPH, C.SS.R., J.C.D., The Dismissal of Religious in Temporary Vows, XIII-220 pp., 1942.
167. PRINCE, REV. JOHN EDWARD, A.B., S.T.B., J.C.D., The Diocesan Chancellor, X-136 pp., 1942.
168. RIESNER, REV. ALBERT JOSEPH, C.SS.R., J.C.D., Apostates and Fugitives from Religious Institutes, IX-168 pp., 1942.
169. STENGER, REV. JOSEPH BERNARD, J.C.D., The Mortgaging of Church Property, 186 pp., 1942.
170. WALDRON, REV. JOSEPH FRANCIS, A.B., J.C.D., The Minister of Baptism, XII-197 pp., 1942.
171. WILLETT, REV. ROBERT ALBERT, J.C.D., The Probative Value of Documents in Ecclesiastical Trials, X-124 pp., 1942.
172. WOEBER, REV. EDWARD MARTIN, M.A., J.C.D., The Interpellations, XII-161 pp., 1942.
173. BENKO, REV. MATTHEW ALOYSIUS, O.S.B., M.A., J.C.D., The Abbot *Nullius*, XVI-148 pp., 1943.
174. CHRIST, REV. JOSEPH JAMES, M.A., S.T.L., J.C.D., Dispensation from Vindicative Penalties, XIV-285 pp., 1943.

175. CLANCY, REV. PATRICK M. J., O.P., A.B., S.T.Lr., J.C.D., The Local Religious Superior, X-229 pp., 1943.
176. CLARKE, REV. THOMAS JAMES, J.C.D., Parish Societies, XII-147 pp., 1943.
177. CONNOLLY, REV. JOHN PATRICK, S.T.L., J.C.D., Synodal Examiners and Parish Priest Consultors, X-223 pp., 1943.
178. DRUMM, REV. WILLIAM MARTIN, A.B., J.C.D., Hospital Chaplains, XII-175 pp., 1943.
179. FLANAGAN, REV. BERNARD JOSEPH, A.B., S.T.L., J.C.D., The Canonical Erection of Religious Houses, X-147 pp., 1943.
180. KELLEHER, REV. STEPHEN JOSEPH, A.B., S.T.B., J.C.D., Discussions with Non-Catholics: Canonical Legislation, X-93 pp., 1943.
181. LEWIS, REV. GORDIAN, C.P., J.C.D., Chapters in Religious Institutes, XII-169 pp., 1943.
182. MARX, REV. ADOLPH, J.C.D., The Declaration of Nullity of Marriages Contracted Outside the Church, X-151 pp., 1943.
183. MATULENAS, REV. RAYMOND ANTHONY, O.S.B., A.B., J.C.D., Communication, a Source of Privileges, XII-225 pp., 1943.
184. O'LEARY, REV. CHARLES GERARD, C.SS.R., J.C.D., Religious Dismissed After Perpetual Profession, X-213 pp., 1943.
185. POWER, REV. CORNELIUS MICHAEL, J.C.D., The Blessing of Cemeteries, XII-231 pp., 1943.
186. SHUHLER, REV. RALPH VINCENT, O.S.A., J.C.D., Privileges of Religious to Absolve and Dispense, XII-195 pp., 1943.
187. ZIOLKOWSKI, REV. THADDEUS STANISLAUS, A.B., J.C.D., The Consecration and Blessing of Churches, XII-151 pp., 1943.
188. HENEGHAN, REV. JOHN JOSEPH, S.T.D., J.C.D., The Marriages of Unworthy Catholics: Canons 1065 and 1066, XVI-213 pp., 1944.
189. CARROLL, REV. COLEMAN FRANCIS, M.A., S.T.L., J.C.L., Charitable Institutions.
190. CIESLUK, REV. JOSEPH EDWARD, PH.B., S.T.L., J.C.L., National Parishes in the United States.
191. COBURN, REV. VINCENT PAUL, A.B., J.C.D., Marriages of Conscience, XII-172 pp., 1944.
192. CONNORS, REV. CHARLES PAUL, C.S.SP., A.B., J.C.D., Extra-Judicial Procurators in the Code of Canon Law, X-94 pp., 1944.
193. COYLE, REV. PAUL RAYMOND, A.B., J.C.D., Judicial Exceptions, X-142 pp., 1944.
194. FAIR, REV. BARTHOLOMEW FRANCIS, A.B., S.T.L., J.C.D., The Impediment of Abduction, XII-122 pp., 1944.
195. GALLAGHER, REV. THOMAS RAPHAEL, O.P., A.B., S.T.LR., J.C.D., The Examination of the Qualities of the Ordinand, X-166 pp., 1944.
196. GANNON, REV. JOHN MARK, S.T.L., J.C.D., The Interstices Required for the Promotion to Orders, XII-100 pp., 1944.

197. Goldsmith, Rev. J. William, B.C.S., S.T.L., J.C.D., The Competence of Church and State Over Marriages—Disputed Points, X-128 pp., 1944.
198. Goodwine, Rev. Joseph Gerard, A.B., S.T.B., J.C.D., The Reception of Converts, XIV-326 pp., 1944.
199. Kowalski, Rev. Romuald Eugene, O.F.M., A.B., J.C.D., Sustenance of Religious Houses of Regulars, X-174 pp., 1944.
200. McCoy, Rev. Alan Edward, O.F.M., J.C.D., Force and Fear in Relation to Delictual Imputability and Penal Responsibility, XII-160 pp., 1944.
201. McDevitt, Rev. Vincent John, Ph.B., S.T.L., J.C.L., Perjury.
202. Martin, Rev. Thomas Owen, Ph.D., S.T.D., J.C.D., Adverse Possession, Prescription and Limitation of Actions: The Canonical "Praescriptio," XX-208 pp., 1944.
203. Miklosovic, Rev. Paul John, A.B., J.C.L., Attempted Marriages and Their Consequent Juridic Effects.
204. Mundy, Rev. Thomas Maurice, A.B., S.T.L., J.C.D., The Union of Parishes, X-164 pp., 1944.
205. O'Dea, Rev. John Coyle, A.B., J.C.D., The Matrimonial Impediment of Nonage, VIII-126 pp., 1944.
206. Olalia, Rev. Alexander Ayson, S.T.L., J.C.D., A Comparative Study of the Christian Constitution of States and the Constitution of the Philippine Commonwealth, XII-136 pp., 1944.
207. Poisson, Rev. Pierre-Marie, C.S.C., A.B., Ph.L., Th.L., J.C.L., Droits Patrimoniaux des Maisons et des Eglises Religieuses.
208. Stadalnikas, Rev. Casimir Joseph, M.I.C., J.C.D., Reservation of Censures, X-141 pp., 1944.
209. Sullivan, Rev. Eugene Henry, S.T.L., J.C.D., Proof of the Reception of the Sacraments, X-165 pp., 1944.
210. Vaughan, Rev. William Edward, J.C.D., Constitutions for Diocesan Courts, X-210 pp., 1944.
211. Paro, Rev. Gino, S.T.D., J.C.L., The Right of Apostolic Legation.
212. Balzer, Rev. Ralph Francis, C.P., J.C.D., The Computation of Time in a Canonical Novitiate, X-227 pp., 1945.
213. Dougherty, Rev. John Whelan, A.B., S.T.L., J.C.D., De Inquisitione Speciali, XII-195 pp., 1945.
214. Dziob, Rev. Michael Walter, J.C.D., The Sacred Congregation for the Oriental Church, XII-181 pp., 1945.
215. Eidenschink, Rev. John Albert, O.S.B., B.A., J.C.D., The Election of Bishops in the Letters of Pope Gregory the Great, VIII-200 pp., 1945.
216. Gill, Rev. Nicholas, C.P., J.C.D., The Spiritual Prefect in Clerical Religious Houses of Study, X-140 pp., 1945.
217. Hynes, Rev. Harry Gerard, S.T.L., J.C.D., The Privileges of Cardinals, XII-183 pp., 1945.
218. McDevitt, Rev. Gerald Vincent, S.T.L., J.C.D., The Renunciation of an Ecclesiastical Office, XIV-179 pp., 1945.

219. MANNING, REV. JOSEPH LEROY, J.C.D., The Free Conferral of Offices, VII-116 pp., 1945.

220. MEYER, REV. LOUIS G., O.S.B., A.B., S.T.B., J.C.D., Alms-gathering by Religious, XII-163 pp., 1945.

221. O'DONNELL, REV. CLETUS FRANCIS, M.A., J.C.D., The Marriage of Minors, XII-268 pp., 1945.

222. PRUNSKIS, REV. JOSEPH, J.C.D., Comparative Law, Ecclesiastical and Civil, in Lithuanian Concordat, X-161 pp., 1945.

223. SWEENEY, REV. FRANCIS PATRICK, C.SS.R., J.C.D., The Reduction of Clerics to the Lay State, X-199 pp., 1945.

224. VOGELPOHL, REV. HENRY JOHN, J.C.D., The Simple Impediments to Holy Orders, XVI-190 pp., 1945.

225. BROCKHAUS, REV. THOMAS AQUINAS, O.S.B., J.C.D., Religious who are known as *Conversi,* X-127 pp., 1945.

226. GRIESE, REV. ORVILLE NICHOLAS, S.T.D., J.C.D., The Marriage Contract and the Procreation of Offspring, XVI-224 pp., 1946.

227. BOUDREAUX, REV. WARREN LOUIS, J.C.L., The *"ab acatholicis nati"* of Canon 1099, § 2.

228. BOWE, REV. THOMAS JOSEPH, A.B., J.C.L., Religious Superioresses.

229. DIEDERICHS, REV. MICHAEL FERDINAND, S.C.J., J.C.D., The Jurisdiction of the Latin Ordinaries over their Oriental Subjects, XIV-153 pp., 1946.

230. DINGMAN, REV. MAURICE JOHN, A.B., S.T.L., J.C.L., The Plaintiff in Contentious Trials.

231. FRISON, REV. BASIL, C.M.F., M.MUS., J.C.D., The Retroactivity of Law, X-221 pp., 1946.

232. GALVIN, REV. WILLIAM ANTHONY, M.A., J.C.D., The Administrative Transfer of Pastors, XII-288 pp., 1946.

233. GORACY, REV. JOSEPH C., J.C.L., The Diriment Matrimonial Impediment of Major Orders.

234. HALE, REV. JOSEPH FRANCIS, M.A., S.T.L., J.C.L., The Pastor of Burial.

235. HENRY, REV. JOSEPH ARTHUR, A.B., J.C.D., The Mass and Holy Communion: Interritual Law, XII-138 pp., 1946.

236. LINENBERGER, REV. HERBERT, C.PP.S., J.C.L., The False Denunciation of an Innocent Confessor.

237. LOWRY, REV. JAMES MARTIN, A.B., J.C.D., Dispensation from Private Vows, XII-216 pp., 1946.

238. LYNCH, REV. GEORGE EDWARD, A.B., S.T.L., J.C.D., Coadjutors and Auxiliaries of Bishops, X-107 pp., 1947.

239. LYNCH, REV. TIMOTHY, M.S.SS.T., J.C.D., Contracts between Bishops and Religious Congregations, XIII-232 pp., 1946.

240. MCCLUNN, REV. JUSTIN DAVID, A.B., S.T.L., J.C.D., Administrative Recourse, VII-142 pp., 1946.

241. LOHMULLER, REV. MARTIN NICHOLAS, A.B., J.C.D., The Promulgation of Law, XII-140 pp., 1947.
242. McGRATH, REV. JAMES, A.B., J.C.D., The Privilege of the Canon, XII-156 pp., 1946.
243. MARBACH, REV. JOSEPH FRANCIS, A.B., J.C.D., Marriage Legislation for the Catholics of the Oriental Rites in the United States and Canada, XIV-314 pp., 1946.
244. SHIMKUS, REV. BERNARD ALOYSIUS, A.B., J.C.L., The Determination and Transfer of Rite.
245. SMITH, REV. VINCENT MICHAEL, A.B., S.T.L., J.C.L., Ignorance Affecting Matrimonial Consent.
246. WACHTRLE, REV. PAUL ANTHONY, A.B., J.C.L., The Baptism of the Children of Non-Catholics.
247. CROTTY, REV. MATTHEW M., J.C.L., The Recipient of First Holy Communion.
248. EAGLETON, REV. GEORGE, J.C.L., The Quinquennial Faculties, Formula IV.
249. GIBBONS, REV. MARION L., C.M., LL.B., J.C.L., Domicile of the Wife Unlawfully Separated from Her Husband.
250. KELLY, REV. BERNARD M., S.T.L., J.C.L., The Functions Reserved to Pastors.
251. KILCULLEN, REV. THOMAS J., LL.M., J.C.L., The Collegiate Moral Person as Party Litigant.
252. LAFONTAINE, REV. GERMAIN J., W.F., J.C.L., Relations Canoniques entre Le Missionnaire et Ses Superieurs.
253. LANE, REV. LORAS T., A.B., S.T.L., J.C.L., Matrimonial Procedure in the Ordinary Court of Second Instance.
254. LOVER, REV. JAMES F., C.SS.R., M.A., J.C.L., The Master of Novices.
255. McNICHOLAS, REV. TIMOTHY J., J.C.L., The *Septimae manus* Witness.
256. MAROSITZ, REV. JOSEPH J., M.S.C., J.C.L., Obligations and Privileges of Religious Promoted to the Episcopal or Cardinalitial Dignities.
257. MURPHY, REV. FRANCIS J., A.B., J.C.L., Legislative Powers of the Provincial Council.
258. O'BRIEN, REV. ROMAEUS W., O. Carm., J.C.L., The Provincial Superior in Religious Orders of Men.
259. PFALLER, REV. BENEDICT A., O.S.B., J.C.L., The *Ipso facto* Effected Dismissal of Religious.
260. POPEK, REV. ALPHONSE S., M.A., J.C.L., The Rights and Obligations of Metropolitans.
261. RISTUCCIA, REV. BERNARD J., C.M., J.C.L., Quasi-Religious.
262. SONNTAG, REV. NATHANIEL L., O.F.M. Cap., J.C.L., Censorship of Special Classes of Books.
263. STADLER, REV. JOSEPH N., J.C.L., Frequent Holy Communion.
264. SZAL, REV. IGNATIUS J., J.C.L., The Communication of Catholics with Schismatics.
265. WAGNER, REV. URBAN S., O.F.M. Conv., J.C.L., Parochial Substitute Vicars and Supplying Priests.

www.ingramcontent.com/pod-product-compliance
Lightning Source LLC
LaVergne TN
LVHW050230080826
844660LV00012B/505

* 9 7 8 0 8 1 3 2 2 4 3 2 9 *